Letters of John Fletcher

Letters of John Fletcher

Selected and Edited by Edward Cook

Kingsley Press
Shoals, Indiana

Letters of John Fletcher

Published by Kingsley Press
PO Box 973
Shoals, IN 47581
USA
Tel. (800) 971-7985
www.kingsleypress.com
E-mail: sales@kingsleypress.com

ISBN: 978-1-937428-47-1 (paperback)
ISBN: 978-1-937428-44-0 (eBook)

First Kingsley Press edition 2014

This Kingsley Press edition is a reprint of the paperback edition of 1999 produced by Harvey Christian Publishers and is published with their permission.

Contents

Important Dates in the Life of John Fletcher

Born	Sept. 12, 1729
Entered Military Service	1749
Became Tutor at Tern Hall, England	1752
Converted. Joined Methodist Society	1755
Ordained in the Church of England	1757
Installed as Vicar of Madeley	1760
Visited France, Italy, Switzerland	1769
Installed at Trevecca	1770
Visited Switzerland for Health Reasons	1777
Returned to Madeley from Switzerland	1781
Married to Mary Bosanquet	Nov. 12, 1781
Died	Aug. 14, 1785

Foreword

THE letters of John Fletcher which comprise this volume are selected from two sources. By far the greater part are taken from a collection of writings edited by the Rev. Melvill Horne, the clergyman who succeeded Mr. Fletcher as Vicar of Madeley (*Posthumous Pieces of the Late Reverend John William De La Fletchere*, Third Edition, Dublin, 1802). The remainder are taken from the biography by Joseph Benson (*The Life of the Rev. John W. De La Fletchere*, New York, 1855).

The editor of the former volume states in his preface that "a large part of the letters is transcribed from the originals, others from authentic copies, and some from a small collection of letters published a few years ago in Dublin." As well as letters, Mr. Horne's edition also contains several pieces which he refers to as "fragments." A number of these seem to be in the form of written sermons or exhortations. We have included a number of these so-called "fragments" at the end of this volume under the heading "Miscellaneous Writings." Rev. Horne says that these were in the author's manuscript, transcribed by Mrs. Fletcher from some of his old pocket books.

Choosing what to put in and what to leave out of such a volume as this has been difficult. Our aim (perhaps not always achieved) has been to retain that which is devotional and spiritually instructive, and to leave out much that is merely incidental and historical—especially those things which would have been of interest only to Mr. Fletcher's near contemporaries. On this principle, sometimes whole letters have been omitted, while others have been abridged. Ellipses usually indicate where material has been left out.

Very few liberties have been taken by the editor. Alterations have usually been limited to the shortening of paragraphs and sentences, with perhaps the introduction of a word or two here and there to improve the flow. Some awkward grammatical constructions and old usages have also been updated, but we stress that this has been done with great caution, and with the sole motive of improving readability. (The practice of modern editors taking the liberty to substantially alter and paraphrase old writings is something of which we do not, on the whole, approve.) Punctuation has been modernized, and American English spelling has been used throughout.

Various methods of presenting the letters have been suggested, but we decided that the most straightforward way would be to present them in chronological order.

My deep gratitude is extended to Mrs. Lillian Harvey, who decided many years ago that such a book as this should be published, and entrusted me with the preparation of it for the press. I am grateful for her inspiration, encouragement, and most of all her support in prayer. I am also indebted to Bruce Garrison for kindly loaning me his copy of the book by Melvill Horne before he himself had had a chance to read it.

Our hope and prayer is that you will be as challenged and inspired in the reading as we have been in the preparation.

Edward Cook
Kingsley Press
June 2014

Introduction

I WENT to see a man that had one foot in the grave; but I found a man that had one foot in Heaven!" So wrote a visitor to the sick bed of John Fletcher of Madeley. Indeed, so heavenly-minded and so saintly was this clergyman from Switzerland that his closest associates all agreed that they had never met his equal.

Our purpose in this short introduction is not to sketch Mr. Fletcher's life, as this has been done elsewhere.[1] Rather we wish to take a brief look at the impact his life had on some of his contemporaries—mostly close friends or colleagues—as expressed in their own words. His humility was such that he rarely spoke of himself, and any good that issued from his life he would certainly have attributed, not to himself, but to the indwelling Christ. The following testimonies to his saintliness must be viewed in that light.

We begin with John Wesley, the founder of Methodism. In concluding an address upon the occasion of Mr. Fletcher's death, Wesley stated:

> I was intimately acquainted with him for above thirty years. I conversed with him morning, noon, and night, without the least reserve, during a journey of many hundred miles; and in all that time I never heard him speak one improper word, nor saw him do an improper action.... Many exemplary men have I known, holy in heart and life, within fourscore years, but one equal to him I have not known—one so inwardly and outwardly devoted to God. So unblamable a character in every respect I have not found either in Europe or America, and I scarce expect to find another such on this side of eternity.

And near the end of Wesley's short biography of Mr. Fletcher we find these words:

---

1 Excellent sketches of the lives of both John and Mary Fletcher can be found in *They Knew Their God*, Volume 5, by Lillian G. Harvey, available from Harvey Christian Publishers

> In general it is easy to perceive that a more excellent man has not appeared in the Church for some ages. It is true, in several ages, and in several countries, many men have excelled in particular virtues and graces. But who can point out, in any age or nation, one that so highly excelled in all—one that was enabled in so large a measure to "put on the whole armor of God?" yea, so to "put on Christ," as to "perfect holiness in the fear of God?"

It is no secret that John Fletcher was, in the words of Luke Tyerman, "Wesley's designated successor" as leader of the Methodists. As it happened, Wesley outlived him by six years!

James Ireland, an intimate friend and regular correspondent of Mr. Fletcher, paid the following tribute:

> I never saw Fletcher's equal. On him great grace was bestowed. What deadness to the world! What spiritual mindedness! What zeal for souls! What communion with God! What intercourse with Heaven! What humility at the feet of Jesus! What moderation towards all men! What love to the poor! In short, he possessed the mind which was in Christ Jesus.

The Rev. Mr. Gilpin, a close friend and associate of Mr. Fletcher, and one of his biographers, wrote of him:

> He outran the most zealous of his companions. He overtook many who were steadily persevering in the path of life, and appeared at the head of those who were pressing after the highest attainable state of sanctity and grace. From the commencement to the conclusion of his pilgrimage, there was never once perceived in him the least imaginable tendency to a loitering or lukewarm disposition. If he was not every moment actually upon the stretch after spiritual improvement, he was observed, at least, with "his loins girded, his shoes on his feet, and his staff in his hand." The fervor of his spirit was a silent but sharp reproof to the negligent and unfaithful.

Even those who held very different theological views from Mr. Fletcher could not help admitting that he was possessed of an extraordinary degree of piety. The Rev. Henry Venn, who strongly differed with him on several points of doctrine, yet had this to say about his godly character:

> He was a luminary; a *luminary* did I say? He was a *sun*. I have known all the great men for these fifty years; but I have known none like him. I was intimately acquainted with him, and was under the same roof with him once for six weeks, during which time I never heard him say a single word which was not proper to be spoken, and which had not a tendency to "minister grace to the hearers."

To these various testimonies regarding Mr. Fletcher's godly character we add a few words from one who was more intimate than any—his wife Mary: "Never did I behold anyone more dead to the things of the world. His treasure was above; and so was his heart also."

—oOo—

There have been some, in most ages of Christianity and in most countries where it is professed, who have emulated its primitive and genuine excellence. Among these exalted few, the subject of the biography[2] *before us is unquestionably to be ranked. In whatever period he had lived, to whatever department of Christians he had belonged, he would have shone in the religious hemisphere as a star of the first magnitude.*

—Eclectic Review, 1805

2 *The Life of the Rev. John W. De La Fletchere*, by Joseph Benson.

Selected Letters

I have been looking over many of his letters, and observe in them all, what I have a thousand times observed in his conversation and behavior, the plainest marks of every Christian—grace and virtue.

—Joseph Benson

To John Wesley

London, May 26, 1757

Rev Sir—If I did not write to you before Mrs. Wesley had asked me, it was not that I wanted a remembrancer within, but rather an encourager without. There is generally such a sense of my own unworthiness upon my heart that I sometimes dare hardly open my mouth before a child of God; and I think it an unspeakable honor to stand before one who has recovered something of the image of God, or sincerely seeks after it. Is it possible that such a sinful worm as I should have the privilege to converse with one whose soul is sprinkled with the blood of my Lord? The thought amazes me, confounds me, and fills my eyes with tears of humble joy...

I rejoice that you find every where an increase of praying souls. I doubt not but the prayer of the righteous hath great power with God, and cannot but believe that it must tend to promote the fulfilling of Christ's gracious promises to His Church. He must, and certainly will come, at the time appointed; for He is not slack, as some men count slackness. Although He would have all to come to repentance, yet He has not forgotten to be true and just. Only He will come with more mercy, and will increase the light that shall be at evening-tide, according to His promise in Zech. 14:7. I should rather think that the visions are not yet plainly disclosed, and that the day and year in which the Lord will begin to make bare His arm openly are still concealed from us.

I must say of Mr. Walsh, as he once said to me concerning God, "I wish I could attend him every where, as Elisha did Elijah." But since the will of God calls me from him, I must submit and drink the cup prepared for me. I have not seen him, unless for a few moments, three or four times before divine service. We must either meet at the Throne of Grace or meet but seldom. O when will the communion of saints be complete! Lord, hasten the time, and let me have a place among them that love Thee and one another in sincerity.

I set out in two days for the country. O may I be faithful: harmless like a dove, wise like a serpent, and bold as a lion for the common cause! O Lord, do not forsake me! Stand by the weakest of Thy servants, and enable Thy children to bear with me and wrestle with Thee in my behalf. O bear with me, dear Sir, and give me your blessing every day, and the Lord will return it to you sevenfold. I am, Rev. and dear Sir, your unworthy servant.

To Mrs. Glynne

London, April 18, 1758

Madam—As it is never too late to do what multiplicity of business—rather than forgetfulness—has forced us to defer, I am not ashamed, though after some months, to use the liberty you gave me to inquire after the welfare of your soul. I am conscious I have not forgotten you at the Throne of Grace. O may my petitions have reached Heaven and forced from thence at least some drops of those spiritual showers of righteousness, peace, and joy in the Holy Ghost which I implore for you.

Though I trust the unction from above teaches you all things needful to salvation, especially the necessity of continuing instant in prayer and watching thereunto with all perseverance, yet I think it my duty to endeavor to add wings to your desires after holiness by enforcing them with mine. O were I but clothed with all the righteousness of Christ, my prayers would avail much; and the lukewarmness of my brethren would not increase my guilt, as being myself an instance of that coldness of love which puts me upon interceding for them.

Though I speak of lukewarmness, I do not accuse you, Madam, of having given way to it. On the contrary, it is my duty and the joy of my heart to hope that you stir up more and more the gift of God which is in you; that the evidences of your interest in a bleeding Lord become clearer every day; that the love of Christ constrains you more and more to deny yourself, take up your cross in all things, and follow Him patiently, through bad and good report. In a word, that continually leaving the things which are behind, you stretch forward, through sunshine or darkness, toward the prize of your high calling in Jesus Christ—I mean a heart emptied of pride and filled with all the fullness of God.

I have often thought of you, Madam, in reading the letters of a lady who was a Christian—an eminent Christian—not to say one of the brightest lights that God has raised since the late revival of godliness. The reproach of Christ was her crown of rejoicing, His cross her continual support, His followers her nearest companions, His example the pattern of her conversation. She lived a saint and died an angel. O when shall I write as she did? When my heart shall be as full of God as hers was.

May the Lord enable you to walk in her steps and grant me to see you shining among the humble, loving Marys of this age, as she did but a few months ago. Her God is our God. The same Spirit that animated her is waiting at the door of our hearts—waiting to cleanse them and fill them with His consolations, if we will but exclude the world and let Him in. Why should we then give way to despondency and refuse to cherish that lively hope, which, if any one has, he will purify himself even as God is pure? Take courage then, Madam, and consider that the hour of self-denial and painful wrestling with God will be short, and the time of victorious recompense as long as eternity itself. May the Lord enable you and me to consider this well and to act accordingly.

I conclude by commending you to the Lord, and to the word of His grace. Recommending myself to your prayers, I am, Madam, your obedient servant for Christ's sake.

To Charles Wesley

London, March 22, 1759

My Dear Sir— ... Since your departure, I have lived more than ever like a hermit. It seems to me that I am an unprofitable weight upon the earth. I want to hide myself from all. I tremble when the Lord favors me with a sight of myself. I tremble to think of preaching only to dishonor God. Tomorrow I preach at West Street with all the feelings of Jonah. O would to God I might be attended with success! If the Lord shall in any degree sustain my weakness, I shall consider myself as indebted to your prayers.

A proposal has lately been made to me, to accompany Mr. Nathaniel Gilbert to the West Indies. I have weighed the matter. On one hand I feel that I have neither sufficient zeal, nor grace, nor talents, to expose myself to the temptations and labors of a mission in the West Indies. But, on the other hand, I believe that if God call me thither, the time is not yet come. I wish to be certain that I am converted myself, before I leave my converted brethren to convert heathens.

Pray let me know what you think of this business. If you condemn me to put the sea between us, the command would be a hard one; but I might possibly prevail on myself to give you that proof of the deference I pay to your judicious advice...

I have taken possession of my little hired chamber; there I have outward peace, and I wait for that which is within. I was this morning with Lady Huntingdon, who salutes you... Our conversation was deep, and full of the energy of faith on the part of the Countess. As to me, I sat like Saul at the feet of Gamaliel.

To Charles Wesley

London, April, 1759

My Dear Sir—With an heart bowed down with grief, and eyes bathed with tears, occasioned by our late heavy loss—I mean the death of Mr. Walsh—I take my pen to pray you to intercede for me. What! that sincere, laborious, and zealous servant of God! Was he saved only as by fire, and was not his prayer heard till the twelfth hour was just expiring? O where shall I appear—I who am an unprofitable servant? Would to God my eyes were fountains of water to weep for my sins! Would to God I might pass the rest of my days in crying, "Lord have mercy upon me!" All is vanity—grace, talents, labors—if we compare them with the mighty stride we have to take from time to eternity! Lord, remember me now that Thou art in Thy Kingdom!

I have preached and administered the sacrament at West Street sometimes in the holidays. May God water the poor seed I have sown and give it fruitfulness, though it be only in one soul!

I have lately seen so much weakness in my heart, both as a minister and a Christian, that I know not which is most to be pitied—the man, the believer, or the preacher. Could I at last be truly humbled, and continue so always, I should esteem myself happy in making this discovery. I preach merely to keep the chapel open, until God shall send a workman after His own heart. If I did not know myself a little better than I did formerly, I should tell you that I had ceased altogether from placing any confidence in my repentances, etc. But I see my heart is so full of deceit that I cannot depend on my knowledge of myself…

The day Mr. Walsh died, the Lord gave our brethren the spirit of prayer and supplication; many unutterable groans were offered up for him at Spitalfields, where I was. Who shall render us the same kind office? Is not our hour near? O my God, when Thou comest, prepare us, and we shall be ready! You owe your children an elegy upon his death, and you cannot employ your poetic talents on a better subject…

TO CHARLES WESLEY

Tern Hall, July 19, 1759

MY DEAR SIR—Instead of apologizing for my silence, I will tell you that I have twenty times endeavored to break it, but without effect. I will simply relate the cause of it, referring you to the remembrance of your own temptations for that patience you must exercise towards a weak, tempted soul. This is the fourth summer that I have been brought hither, in a peculiar manner, to be tempted of the devil in a wilderness. I have improved so little by my past exercises that I have not defended myself better than in the first year.

Being arrived here, I began to spend my time as I had determined—one part in prayer, and the other in meditation on the holy Scriptures. The Lord blessed my devotions. I advanced from conquering to conquer, leading every thought captive to the obedience of Jesus Christ, when it pleased God to show me some of the folds of my heart. As I looked for nothing less than such a discovery, I was extremely surprised; so much so, as to forget Christ. You may judge already what was the consequence. A spiritual languor seized on all the powers of my soul, and I suffered myself to be carried away quietly by a current, the rapidity of which I was unacquainted with.

Neither doubt nor despair troubled me for a moment; my temptation took another course. It appeared to me that God would be much more glorified by my damnation than by my salvation. It seemed altogether incompatible with the holiness, the justice, and the veracity of the Supreme Being, to admit so stubborn an offender into His presence. I could do nothing but stand astonished at the patience of God…

Yesterday, however, as I sang one of your hymns, the Lord lifted up my head and commanded me to face my enemies. By His grace I am already conqueror, and I doubt not but I shall soon be more than conqueror. Although I deserve it not, nevertheless, hold up my hands till all these Amalekites be put to flight.

To Charles Wesley

London, September 14, 1759

My Dear Sir— … Your last lines drew tears from my eyes. I cannot wait till your death to beseech you to give me that benediction of which you speak. I conjure you, in the name of Christ, to give it me when you read these lines, and to repeat it as often as you think of a poor brother who needs the prayers of every one, and who cannot part with yours.

I accept with pleasure the obliging proposal you make me for the approaching winter; and I entreat you to consider it less as a proposal than as an engagement into which you have entered, and of which I have a right to solicit the fulfillment. Permit me only to add to it one condition, which is to make our reading, etc. tend, as much as possible, to that poverty of spirit which I so greatly need.

A few days ago, the Lord gave me two or three lessons on that subject, but alas! how have I forgotten them! I saw—I felt—that I was entirely void of wisdom and virtue. I was ashamed of myself and could say, with a degree of feeling which I cannot describe, "I do nothing, have nothing, am nothing; I crawl in the dust." I could then say what Gregory Lopez was enabled to say at all times, "There is no man of whom I have not a better opinion than of myself." I could have placed myself under the feet of the most atrocious sinner and have acknowledged him for a saint in comparison of myself.

If ever I am humble and patient, if ever I enjoy solid peace of mind, it must be in this very spirit. Ah! why do I not actually find these virtues? Because I am filled with self-sufficiency. I am possessed by that self-esteem which blinds me and hinders me from doing justice to my own demerits. O! pray that the Spirit of Jesus may remove these scales from my eyes for ever and compel me to retire into my own nothingness.

To what a monstrous idea had you well nigh given birth! What! the labors of my ministry under you deserve a salary! Alas! I have done nothing but dishonor God hitherto, and am not in a condition to do any thing else for the future! If then I am permitted to stand in the courts of the Lord's house, is it not for me to make an acknowledgment rather than to receive one? If I ever receive any thing of the Methodist Church, it shall be only as an indigent mendicant receives alms, without which he would perish...

I have great need of your advice relative to the letters which I receive one after another from my relations, who unite in their invitations to me to return to my own country. One says, to settle my affairs there; another, to preacher there; and a third, to assist him to die, etc. They press me to declare whether I renounce my family and the demands I have upon it. My mother desires that I will at least go and see her, and commands me to do so in the strongest terms.

What answer shall I make? If she thought as you do, I should write to her, "Where the Christians are, there is my country." "My mother, my brethren, my sisters, are those who do the will of my Heavenly Father." She is not in a state of mind to digest such an answer; a mother is a mother long.

On the other hand, I have no inclination to yield to their desires—which appear to me merely natural—for I shall lose precious time and incur expense. My presence is not absolutely necessary to my concerns; and it is more probable that my relations will pervert me to vanity and interest, than that I shall convert them to genuine Christianity. Lastly, I shall have no opportunity to exercise my ministry. Our Swiss ministers, who preach only once a week, will not look upon me with a more favorable eye than the ministers here. Irregular preaching is impracticable and would only cause me either to be laid in prison or immediately banished from the country.

How does your family do? May the Almighty be your defence day and night! What He protects is well protected. Permit me to thank you for the sentence from Kempis, with which you close your letter, by returning to you another: "You run no risk in considering yourself as the wickedest of men; but you are in danger if you prefer yourself to any one."

To Charles Wesley

Tern Hall, Sept. 29th, 1759

My Dear Sir— … If I know anything of true brotherly love, which I often doubt, it agrees perfectly well with the love of God, as the sounds of the different parts in music agree with each other. Their union arises from their just difference, and they please so much the more as they appear the more opposed. The opposition of sentiments between divine and brotherly love, together with the subordination of the latter, forms that delightful combat in the soul of a believer, termed by the apostle the being divided between two, which concludes with a sacrifice of resignation such as the natural man is incapable of. Your expression, "Spread the moral sense all o'er," gives me an idea of that charity which I seek.

The love of Gregory Lopez appears to me to have been too stoical. I do not discover in it that vehement desire, those tears of love, that ardor of seeing and possessing each other in the bowels of Jesus Christ, which I find so frequently in the Epistles of St. Paul. If this sensibility be a failing, I do not wish to be exempt from it. What is your opinion?

When I was reading Telemachus with my pupils, I was struck with this expression: "He blushed to have been born with so little feeling for men, and to appear to them so inhuman." I easily applied the first part, and the Son of Ulysses gave me an example of Christian repentance which I wish to follow till my heart is truly circumcised. Send me some remedy, or give me some advice against this hardness of heart under which I groan…

I fear you did not rightly understand what I wrote about the proposal you made me at London. So far from making conditions, I feel myself unworthy of receiving them. Be it what it may, I thank God that I trouble myself with no temporal things. My only fear is that of having too much, rather than too little, of the things necessary for life. I am weary of abundance. I could wish to be poor with my Savior, and those whom He hath chosen to be rich in faith appear to me objects of envy in the midst of their wants. Happy should I be if a secret pride of heart did not disguise itself under these appearances of humility! Happy should I be if that dangerous serpent did not conceal himself under these sweet flowers and feed on their juices.

To Mrs. Royon and Miss Furley

October 1, 1759

My Dear Sisters—I have put off writing to you, lest the action of writing should divert my soul from the awful and delightful worship it is engaged in. But I now conclude I shall be no loser if I invite you to love Him Whom my soul loveth, to dread Him Whom my soul dreadeth, to adore Him Whom my soul adoreth. Sink with me, or rather let me sink with you, before the Throne of Grace; and while cherubim veil their faces, and cry out in tender fear and exquisite trembling, "Holy! holy! holy!" let us put our mouths in the dust and echo back the solemn sound, "Holy! holy! holy!" Let us plunge ourselves into that ocean of purity. Let us try to fathom the depths of divine mercy, and, convinced of the impossibility of such an attempt, let us lose ourselves in them.

Let us be comprehended by God, if we cannot comprehend Him. Let us be supremely happy in God. Let the intenseness of our happiness border on misery, because we can make Him no return. Let our head become water, and our eyes fountains of tears—tears of humble repentance, of solemn joy, of silent admiration, of exalted adoration, of raptured desires, of inflamed transports, of speechless awe. My God, and my all! Your God, and your all! Our God, and our all! Praise Him! With our souls blended in one by divine love, let us with one mouth glorify the father of our Lord Jesus Christ—our Father, Who is over all, through all, and in us all.

I charge you before the Lord Jesus Christ, Who giveth life, and more abundant life; I entreat you, by all the actings of faith, the exertions of hope, the flames of love you ever felt, sink to greater depths of self-abasing repentance, and rise to greater heights of Christ-exalting joy. And let Him Who is able to do exceeding abundantly more than you can ask or think, carry on and fulfill in you the work of faith with power—that power whereby He subdueth all things to Himself. Be steadfast in hope, immovable in patience and love, always abounding in the outward and inward labor of love, and receive the end of your faith, the salvation of your souls.

To the Hon. Mrs. ———

My Dear Friend—To a believer, Jesus is alone the desirable, the everlasting distinction and honor of men. All other advantages, though now so proudly extolled, so vehemently coveted, are, like the down on the thistle, blown away in a moment and never secure to the possessor. Riches are incapable of satisfying. Friends are changeable and precarious. The dear relations who are the delight of our heart are taken away at a stroke. Pain and sickness follow ease and health in quick succession. But amidst all the possible changes of life, Christ is a rock. To see Him by faith, to lay hold, to rely upon Him, to live upon Him, this is the *refuge* from the storm, the *shadow* from the heat. May it be given to you abundantly! And in order to obtain it, nothing more or less is required of you than a full and frequent confession of your own abominable nature and heart. Kneel as a true beggar at the door of mercy, declaring you came there expecting notice and relief only because God our Savior came to redeem incarnate Devils, and, for the glory of His grace, to convert them into saints and servants of the living God—into children of God and heirs of Glory.

I think you take a sure method to perplex yourself if you want to see your own faith, or look for one moment at yourself for proof of your faith. Others must see it in your works, but you must feel it in your heart. The glory of Jesus is now, by faith, realized to the mind in some such manner as an infinitely grand and beautiful object which appears in the firmament of heaven. It arrests and fixes the attention of the spectators on itself. It captivates them and, by the pleasure it imparts, they are led on to view it. So when Jesus is our peace, strength, righteousness, food, salvation, and our all, we are penetrated with a consciousness of it. We should never rest short of this feeling, nor ever think we have it strong enough. This is to *keep the faith*; and our chief conflict and most constant labor must be against our own heart, the things of the world, and the suggestions of our great enemy, who are all intent to divert us from this *One object* which Mary placed herself before—or to make us doubt whether in the life and death of Immanuel there was such unsearchable riches and efficacy, such a complete salvation for all His people, or whether we are in that number. For my own part, I am often tempted to suspect whether I am not speaking great swelling words of Christ, and yet am no more than sounding brass or a tinkling cymbal. I find the only successful way of answering this doubt is immediately to address to Jesus a prayer to this effect: "Whosoever cometh to Thee, Thou wilt in no wise cast out. Lord, have not I come to Thee? Am not I as a brand plucked out of the fire—depending upon Thee for life? See if there be any way of wickedness in me, and lead me in the way everlasting."

My eye looks to the blessed Jesus, my heart longs to be more in His service, my love—O that it were greater toward Him! I mourn deeply for my corruptions, which are many and great. When I look at Him and contemplate His great salvation, I admire, I adore, and, in some measure, I love. But when I look at myself, my heart rises at the sight. Black and devilish, selfish and proud, carnal and covetous, and most abominably unclean, I lack all things which are good. But I have a blessed, blessed Lord—Christ Jesus—in Whom all fullness dwells for me and for the dear friend to whom I am writing—a fullness of pardon, wisdom, holiness, strength, peace, righteousness, and salvation—a fullness of love, mercy, goodness, truth. All this, and a thousand times more than all this, without any worthiness of merit, only for receiving. O blessed free grace of God! O blessed be His name for Jesus Christ! What a gift! and for whom? For you, my dear friend, if you are *without strength,* if you are in your nature *an enemy,* all this is for you. What says the everlasting God? Believe that He gave His Son for sinners; and as *a sinner* believe in Jesus. He came to save the *lost;* then, as a lost soul, believe in Him. He came to cleanse the filthy; then, as *a filthy soul,* believe in Him. And why should we not thus believe? Can God lie? Impossible! Can we have a better foundation to build on than the *promise* and *oath* of *God?*

My dear friend, I know you will not be angry at my preachment. I aim it all at my own heart. I stand more in need of it than you. I always feel my heart refreshed when I am talking or thinking of Jesus. It is a feast to my sinful soul when I am meditating on the glories which compose His blessed name. But O how dark and ignorant, how little, how exceeding little do I know of Him! O Thou light of the world, enlighten my soul! Teach me to know more of Thy infinite and unsearchable riches, Thou great God-man, that I may love Thee with an increasing love, and serve Thee with an increasing zeal, till Thou bringest me to glory!

To Charles Wesley

Madeley, July, 1762

My Dear Sir— ... Three weeks ago I went to Ludlow to the bishop's visitation, thinking the occasion favorable for my purpose. The churchwardens, when we were upon the spot, refused to support me; and the court has paid no regard to my presentation. Thus I have gained some experience, though at my own cost. The sermon did not touch the string with which I was whipped the last visitation, and I afterwards had the boldness to go and dine with the bishop.

Many of my parishioners are strangely disconcerted at my bringing my gown back from Ludlow. [They thought the bishop would have stripped him of it.] The magistrate I mentioned, who, because he acted as judge of the circuit two years ago, believes himself as able a lawyer as Judge Foster, for the present contents himself with threatenings. I met him the other day; and after he had called me Jesuit, etc., and menaced me with his cane, he assured me again that he would soon put down our assemblies. How ridiculous is this impotent rage!

I have attempted to form a society, and, in spite of much opposition and many difficulties, I hope by God's grace to succeed. I preach, I exhort, I pray, etc., but as yet I seem to have cast the net on the wrong side of the ship. Lord Jesus, come Thyself and furnish me with a divine commission! For some months past, I have labored under an insuperable drowsiness. I could sleep day and night. The hours which I ought to employ with Christ on the mountain, I spend like Peter in the garden...

To Charles Wesley

Madeley, August, 1762

My Dear Sir— ... I still have trials of all sorts. First, spiritual ones. My heart is hard; I have not that filial fear, that sweet, humble melting of heart before the Lord which I consider as essential to spiritual Christianity.

Secondly, the opposition made to my ministry increases. A young clergyman who lives in Madeley-Wood, where he has great influence, has openly declared war against me by pasting on the church door a paper in which he charges me with rebellion, schism, and being a disturber of the public peace. He puts himself at the head of the gentlemen of the parish, as they term themselves; and, supported by the Recorder of Wenlock, he is determined to put in force the Conventicle Act against me.

A few weeks ago, the widow who lives in the Rock Church and a young man who read and prayed in my absence were taken up. I attended them before the Justice, and the young clergyman with his troop were present. They called me Jesuit, etc., and the Justice tried to frighten me by saying that he would put the act in force, though we should assemble only in my own house. I pleaded my cause as well as I could; but, seeing he was determined to hear no reason, I told him he must do as he pleased, and that if the Act in question concerned us, we were ready to suffer all its rigors. In his rage, he went the next day to Wenlock and proposed to grant a warrant to have me apprehended; but, as the other Justices were of opinion that the business did not come under their cognizance, but belonged to the Spiritual Court, he was obliged to swallow his spittle alone. The churchwardens talk of putting me in the Spiritual Court for meeting in houses, etc. But, what is worst of all, three false witnesses offer to prove, upon oath, that I am a liar, and that some of my followers, as they are called, have dishonored their profession, to the great joy of our adversaries.

In the midst of these difficulties, I have reason to bless the Lord that my heart is not troubled. Forget me not in your prayers.

To Mr. Vaughan

Madeley, September 4, 1762

Dear Sir—I am very glad to hear that your delight is still in the ways of the Lord, and I trust you will never stop till you find them all pleasantness to you. Fight the good fight of faith; break through all temptations, dejections, wandering, worldly thoughts; through all unprofitable companions, and the backwardness of an unbelieving heart and carnal mind. Struggle, I say, until you touch Jesus and feel healing, comforting virtue proceeding from Him. And when you know clearly the way to Him, repeat the touch till you find He lives in you by the powerful operation of His loving Spirit. Then you will say with St. Paul, "I live the life of God, yet not I, but Christ Who liveth in me."

I rejoice that you inquire where Christ maketh His flock to rest at noon. The rest from the guilt and power of sin you will find only in inward holiness; and this I apprehend to consist in what St. Paul calls the Kingdom of God: "righteousness," which excludes all guilt; "peace," which banishes all fear that hath torment; and "joy," which can no more subsist with doubts, anxiety, and unstableness of mind, than light can subsist with darkness. That there is a state wherein this Kingdom is set up, firmly set up in the heart, you may see by our Lord's Sermon on the Mount, by His priestly prayer in St. John's Gospel, chapter 17, by the Epistle of that Apostle, and various parts of the Epistles of St. Paul and St. James.

To aim aright at this liberty of the children of God requires a continual acting of faith—a naked faith in a naked promise or declaration—such as, "The Son of God was manifested to destroy the works of the devil." "The law of the Spirit of life in Christ Jesus hath made me free from the law of sin and death." "I can do all things through Christ who strengtheneth me." By "a naked faith in a naked promise," I do not mean a bare assent that God is faithful, and that such a promise in the book of God may be fulfilled in me; but rather a bold, hearty, steady venturing of my soul, body, and spirit upon the truth of the promise with an appropriating act. It is mine, because I am a penitent sinner, determined to believe—come what will. Here you must stop the ear of the mind to the suggestions of the serpent, which, were you to reason with him, would be endless, and would soon draw you out of the simple way of that faith by which we are both justified and sanctified.

You must also remember that it is your privilege to go to Christ by such a faith now, and every succeeding moment; and that you are to bring nothing but a distracted, tossed, hard heart—just such a one as you have now. Here lies the grand mistake of many poor but precious souls. They are afraid to believe, lest it should be presumption, because they have not as yet comfort, joy, love, etc., not considering that this is to look for fruit before the tree be planted. Beware, then, of looking for any peace or joy previous to your believing and letting this become uppermost in your mind.

The Lord make you wise as a serpent and harmless as the loving dove. Beware, however, of the serpent's food—dust; and the dove's bane—birdlime, I mean worldly cares. O, my friend, what is the world? A flying shadow. As we fly through, let us lose ourselves in the Eternal Substance. Farewell in the Lord.

To Miss Hatton

Madeley, November 1, 1762

Madam—I thank you for the confidence you repose in the advice of a poor fellow sinner. May the Father of lights direct you through so vile an instrument! If you build all your hopes of Heaven upon Jesus Christ in all His offices, you do not build without a foundation, but upon the true one.

That there is a seal of pardon, and an earnest of our inheritance above, which you are as yet a stranger to, seems clear from the tenor of your letter. Had I been in the place of the gentleman you mention, I would have endeavored to lay it before you as the fruit of faith, and a most glorious privilege, rather than as the root of faith, and a thing absolutely necessary to the being of it.

I believe many people know when they receive faith, and all people when they receive the seal of their pardon. When they believe in Christ, they are justified in the sight of God. When they are sealed by the Spirit, they are fully assured of that justification in their own conscience. Some receive faith and the seal of their pardon in the same instant, as the jailer for example; but others receive faith first, as the dying thief, the woman of Canaan, David, the people of Samaria (Acts. 8:12-16), and the faithful at Ephesus (Eph. 1:13).

Suppose then that God gave you faith, i.e. a hearty trust in the blood of Christ and a sincere closing with Him as your righteousness and your all, while you received the sacrament (which seems to me very probable, by the account you give me), your way is exceeding plain before you. Hold fast your confidence, but do not rest in it. Trust in Christ; and remember He says, "I am the way," not for you to stop, but to run on in Him.

Rejoice to hear that there is a full assurance of faith to be obtained by the seal of God's Spirit, and go on from faith to faith until you are possessed of it. But remember this, and let this double advice prevent your straying to the right or left: First, that you will have reason to suspect the sincerity of your zeal if you lie down easy without the seal of your pardon and the full assurance of faith. Secondly, while you wait for that seal in all the means of grace, beware of being unthankful for the least degree of faith and confidence in Jesus; beware of burying one talent because you have not five; beware of despising the grain of mustard seed because it is not yet a tree.

May the Lord teach you the middle path between resting short of the happiness of "making your calling and election sure," and supposing you are neither called nor chosen, and that God hath not yet truly begun His good work in you. You can never be too bold in believing, provided you still aspire after new degrees of faith and do not use your faith as a cloak for sin. The Lord despises not the day of small things; only beware of resting in small things. Look for the seal and abiding witness of God's Spirit according to the following direction,

> Restless, resigned, for this I wait,
> For this my vehement soul stands still.

As to deep sights of the evil of sin, the more you go on, the more you will see Christ exceeding lovely, and sin exceeding sinful. Therefore, look up to Jesus as a vile and helpless sinner, pleading His promises, and trust Him for the rest; this is going on.

With respect to myself, in many conflicts and troubles of soul, I have consulted many masters of the spiritual life; but divine mercy did not, does not, suffer me to rest upon the word of a fellow-creature. The best advices have often increased my perplexities, and the end was to make me cease from human dependence and wait upon God from the dust of self-despair. To Him, therefore, I desire to point you and myself, in the Person of Jesus Christ. This incarnate God receives weary, perplexed sinners still, and gives them solid rest. He teaches as no man ever taught; His words have spirit and life; nor can He possibly mistake our case. I am, Madam, your fellow servant in the patience and Kingdom of Jesus.

To Miss Hatton

Madeley, January 28, 1763

Dear Madam—I share in the joy which your deliverance from your late trials gives to those who shared in your perplexity. Heaviness may endure for a night, but gladness cometh in the morning; and when it comes after a long, uneasy night, it is doubly welcome, and deserves a double tribute of praises. O be not wanting in that sweet duty! I mean praising from a sense of the divine goodness, love, and patience towards us. Remember that you are brought from darkness to light to show forth the praises of Him Who calleth you; and that your feet are set at liberty for you to run with patience the race of prayer and praise, self-denial and obedience, which the Lord hath set before you.

If you would go on comfortably and steadily for the time to come, beg of the Lord to give you grace to observe the following advice:

1. Live above earthly and creature comforts.
2. Beware of flatness and lukewarmness as this, if not carried immediately to the Lord, ends often in darkness and deadness.
3. Value divine comforts above all things, and prize Christ above all comforts; that, if they should fail, you may still glory in the God of your salvation.
4. Let that which torments others make your happiness—I mean self-denial and renouncing your own will.
5. Be ready to yield with joy to every conviction of the Spirit of God.
6. Be faithful to present grace and aspire after a continual growth.
7. Live the present moment to God, and avoid perplexing yourself about your past or future experience.

By giving up yourself to Christ as you are, and being willing to receive Him now, as He is, leaving all the rest to Him, you will cut up a thousand temptations by the roots!

To Miss Hatton

Madeley, March 14th, 1763

DEAR MADAM—I am glad you persist in taking up your cross and following the Captain of our salvation. You must expect many difficulties. Some of your greatest trials may come from your dearest friends without and your nearest part within. I have always found it profitable to expect the worst, for a temptation foreseen is half overcome. Let us count the cost daily and learn to value all outward things as dung and dross that we may win Christ.

My heart is at present full of an advice which I have just given, with some success, to the Israelites in the wilderness about this place: Spend the time you have hitherto spent in desponding thoughts, in perplexing considerations upon the badness or uncertainty of your state, in feeling after Christ by the prayer of such faith as you have, whether it be dark or luminous, and come now to the Lord Jesus with your present wants, daring to believe that He waits to be gracious to you. Christ is the way, the highway to the Father; and a highway is as free for a sickly beggar as a glorious prince. If it be suggested, you are too presumptuous to intrude without ceremony upon Him that is "glorious in holiness and fearful in praises," answer in looking up to Jesus,

Be it I myself deceive,
Yet *I must, I must* believe

To Mr. Samuel Hatton

Madeley, April 22, 1763

DEAR SIR—I am glad to find by your welcome letter that Jesus is still precious to you. O may He be so an hundredfold more both to me and you! May we live only to show forth His praise, and grow up into Him in all things!

As for me, I have reason to praise God that He gives me patience to throw in my weak line till He gives the word and enables me to cast the net on the right side and enclose a multitude of sinners. The hope of this bears me up above the toils of a night of ignorance, perplexity, and trials of every sort. I find, blessed be God, that all things work together for my good, whether it be success or want of success, joy or grief, sickness or ease, bad or good report—all encourages or humbles me...

I am quite of your opinion about the mischief that some professors (puffed up in their own fleshly minds) do in the Church of Christ under the mask of sanctity. But my Master bids me bear with the tares until the harvest, lest in rooting them up, I should promiscuously pull of the wheat also. As to Mr. Wesley's system of perfection, it tends rather to promote humility than pride, if I may credit his description of it in the following lines:

Now let me gain perfection's height,
Now let me into *nothing* fall,
Be *less than nothing* in my sight,
And feel that Christ is *all in all.*

More than this I do not desire, and I hope that nothing short of this will satisfy either my dear friend or me...

Let us still make the best of our way to the dear Savior, and drop all our particular opinions in His universal, unbounded love; and whereinsoever any of us is wrong the Lord will reveal it unto us. Pray for my flock, and pray for, dear Sir, your sincere friend and affectionate brother in Christ.

To Charles Wesley

Madeley, July 26th, 1763

My Dear Sir—I have for two months waited impatiently for some news of you, but in vain. Are you alive, paralytic, gouty, slothful, or too busy to write a line to your friends at Madeley? If you have not leisure to write a line, write a word: "I am well," or "I am ill." God grant it may be the former!

Every thing is pretty quiet here now. Many of our offenses die away, though not long ago I had trials in abundance. Blessed be the Lord, He gave me His peace. It is not, however, without fighting that I keep it. One of my late trials might have had consequences to make me quit Madeley, and, I praise God, I am ready to do it without looking behind me even this day. The young person I mentioned as being tempted of the devil is happily delivered, and we have had the testimonies of Mr. Mould who preached here three weeks ago, and of Mr. R——, who spent four days here and preached last Sunday. He is an excellent young man, and only wants a little of the Methodist zeal to temper the reserve of Mr. W——.

When will you come to Madeley? What do you do at London? Have you repaired the breach and healed the plague? May the Lord give you all the wisdom, the patience, the zeal, the gentleness, and the health you stand in need of! Ask them for your poor brother.

To Miss Hatton

Madeley, August 3rd, 1763

Dear Madam—I am heartily glad to find that your heart is set upon obtaining the one thing needful, "Christ in us," with all His graces, "the hope of glory." I beg, in my Master's name, you would cherish the conviction of the need of this prize of your high calling and pursue it in the new and living way in which the fathers trod—that of the cross, and that of faith. We travel in the first by continually denying ourselves in the desire of the flesh, the desire of the eye, and the pride of life. We advance in the second by aiming at Christ, claiming Christ, embracing Christ, delighting and rejoicing in Christ received in the heart through the channel of the Gospel promises.

To be able to go on in the way of the cross and of faith, you stand in need, Madam, of much recollection, steady watchfulness over the workings of your own heart, and diligent attention to the whispers of divine grace. That the Lord would powerfully enable us to run on with faith and patience till we inherit the promises is the prayer of, Madam, your servant in Christ.

To Miss Hatton

Madeley, Aug. 19th, 1763

Dear Madam—Mrs. Hatton gave me this morning your serious letter. You wisely observe therein the continual need professing Christians have to guard against religious chit chat, and conclude by requesting a few lines, when I should have an opportunity of writing. But as there is nothing in your letter which *requires* an answer, I was thinking whether I could answer it without being guilty of religious chit chat; for as there is such a thing in speaking, no doubt in writing also. I believe I should have sacrificed to conscience what the world calls good manners had I not just after accidentally opened Lopez's Life upon the following passage, which I shall transcribe, hoping it will be blessed both to the reader and copier.

"He was as sparing of words in writing as in speaking. He never wrote first to any one, nor did he answer others but when necessity or charity obliged him to it; and then so precisely and in so few words that nothing could be retrenched. I have several of his letters in my hands of five or six lines each. In answer to those he had received from the Viceroy of Mexico, he sent him one containing only these words: 'I will do what you command me.' And although this manner of writing might seem disrespectful to persons of so high quality, yet it gave no offence from one who was so far from all compliments and who never spoke anything superfluous."

Now, Madam, for fear of writing anything superfluous, I shall conclude by wishing both you and I may follow Lopez as he followed Christ. I subscribe myself, Madam, the ready servant of you and yours in the Gospel.

To Miss Hatton

Madeley, ——

My Dear Friend in the Lord—I thought last Sunday that you were not far from the Kingdom of God. Had your wisdom stooped a little more to the foolishness of the cross you would have been the little child to whom God reveals what He justly hides from the wise and prudent. I longed to have followed you, and given you no rest till you had drunk the cup of blessing which your Lord hath mixed for you with His bitter tears and most precious blood. And how glad was I to find last night that you had no aversion to Jesus and His love, nor to the simple, foolish way of entertaining Him in your heart, as you can by mere faith. How often since has my heart danced for joy in hope that the time is come that the Lord will fully open your heart, like that of Lydia, to attend, without caviling or objecting, to His still, small voice—"I am thine, and thou art Mine. Fear not, for I have redeemed thee, thou worm Jacob. I have graven thy name (i.e. sinner) upon the palms of My hands. I shall see in thee the travail of My soul, and shall be satisfied. Let Me not upbraid thee longer for willful unbelief and hardness of heart; but believe upon the testimony of My word and servants that I am risen for thy justification. Say not, I must ascend into heaven, or descend into the deep—I must feel first such a height of joy or depth of sorrow. No! Believe simply that the word is nigh thee, in thy mouth and in thy heart, namely the word of faith preached unto thee. I am the Lamb of God. I have carried away thy sins, and I do not condemn thee, though thou condemnest thyself. I am He, that for mine own sake blotteth out thy sins as a cloud and thy iniquities as a thick cloud; because I will have mercy on whom I will have mercy, namely on him who will be saved in my way, by that faith which stumbles the Jew and is foolishness to the Greek, but which will prove to thee both the wisdom and power of God. Fear not, then, O thou of little faith; wherefore shouldest thou doubt any longer? Do I despise the day of small things? Do

I break the bruised reed or quench the smoking flax? Am not I the Good Shepherd who carrieth the lambs in His bosom? Does a mother forsake her sucking child because it is weak, sickly, unable to walk, or even to stand? Yea, though a mother should so forsake her child, yet will I never leave thee nor forsake thee. Only lean on thy Beloved and I will bring thee up out of the wilderness. Abandon thyself wholly to My care and I, the keeper of Israel, will care for thee. Thy business shall be henceforth to repose on My bosom and wash thee in My bleeding heart. My business shall be to carry thee safe through or above all thy enemies. Only remember thy business is to believe and love: and trust Me for a faithful discharge of Mine—to save thee with a high hand."

Thus, my friend, will your dear Savior speak to your heart if you do not drown His voice by the objections of your false wisdom. O down with it! It is the fruit of the tree of death. Away to the tree of life! Take freely, eat and live. I know you are willing through grace; and Christ, Who hath made you willing, is ten thousand times more willing than you. How then can He cast you out? What hinders but that you should, as a spiritual Rebekah, say, "Now and ever, I will have that man"? You go upon a sure bottom—you need not fear being slighted. For in the letter He hath wrote you from Heaven, to invite you to the marriage, He says, "I have betrothed thee to me with everlasting, yea with bleeding kindness." Indeed, indeed He sends me to you, to assure you He is the same yesterday, today, and for ever. And were you the sister of Magdalen in outward wickedness, He sends you word that you may kiss His feet and rejoice that much is forgiven you, even though you should not have one tear to wash them with. His blood, His precious blood hath washed His feet and does wash your heart and will wash it white as snow. O let it be your business to consider it with a believing thought; that is the way to apply it to your heart.

I would have called upon you this morning, had not my intended journey prevented it. Till I have an opportunity of calling, I beg, as upon my knees, you would make use of the following directions, which I think as truly applicable to your state as they are truly evangelical:

(1) It is better to perish for believing wrong than for not believing at all. Venture then, with Esther, "If I perish, I perish." I had rather perish in trying to touch the scepter of grace than in indolently waiting till the King touches me with it.

(2) Christ often reveals Himself as a babe, a feeble infant. Do not despise Him in His lowest, weakest state. Do not say to your Savior, "I will not receive Thee unless Thou appear in a blaze of glorious light." Reject not the little leaven; and if your grain of faith is small as mustard seed, be the more careful not to throw it away as dirt. The Holy Ghost says, "The light of the just shines more and more to the perfect day." How feeble is the light of the early morning; how indiscernible from darkness!

(3) Sin gives you your first title to the Friend of sinners, and a simple naked faith the second. Do not then puzzle yourself about contrition, faithfulness, love, joy, power over sin, and a thousand such things, which the white devil will persuade you that you must bring to Christ. He will receive you gladly with the greatest mountain of sin. The smallest grain of faith, at Christ's feet, will remove that mountain.

(4) At the peril of your soul, desire *at present* neither peace nor joy, nor puzzle yourself even about love. Only desire that this blessed Man may be your Bridegroom, and that you may firmly believe that He is so because He hath given you His flesh and blood upon the cross. Continue believing this and trusting in Him.

(5) You have nothing to do with sin and self, although they will have much to do with you. Your business is with Jesus, with His free, unmerited love, with His glorious promises, etc.

(6) Strongly expect no good from your own heart. Expect nothing but unbelief, hardness, unfaithfulness, and backsliding. And when you find them there, be not shaken nor discouraged; rather rejoice that you are to live by faith on the faithful heart of Christ, and cast not away your confidence, which hath great recompense of reward.

(7) When you are dull and heavy, as will often be the case, remember to live on Christ and claim the more by naked faith. I have not time to say more; but Jesus, Whom you hold by the hem of His promise, will teach you all the day long. Look unto Him and be saved, and remember that He forgives seventy times seven. May His dawning love attend you till it is noonday in your soul. Pray for him who earnestly prays for you—I mean your unworthy servant.

To Mrs. Glynne

Madeley, Sept. 2nd, 1763

Dear Madam—... If the Father of lights hath drawn your soul in any warmer desires after the glorious sense of His love, and enabled you to sit down and count the cost, and give up *fully* whatever may have a tendency to keep you out of the delightful enjoyment of the pearl of great price, I shall rejoice greatly; for it is my hearty desire that all my Christian friends and I might grow up daily towards the measure of the full stature of Christ.

I return you my most affectionate thanks, Madam, for your book, and for the franks you added to it. May you use all the promises of the gospel as franks from Jesus to send momentary petitions to Heaven, and may an unwearied faith be the diligent messenger!

What proved a disappointment to you was none to me, having been forced by many such disappointments to look for comfort in nothing but these comprehensive words—*Thy will be done*! A few more trials will convince you, experimentally, of the heavenly balm they contain to sweeten the pains and heal the wounds that crosses and afflictions may cause. We often improve more by one hour's resignation than by a month's reading; and when we can exercise neither gifts nor graces, one of the last is always excepted—*Patience*—which is then worth all the rest.

O let us make the best of our day, Madam!—a day of grace—a Gospel day—a day of health—a precarious day of life! Let us believe, hope, love, obey, repent, spend and be spent for Him Who hath loved us unto death.

Mr. M. said your portmanteau would go today; but whether it goes or stays, let neither wind nor tide keep us back from Jesus Christ. That His love may fill our hearts is the repeated wish of, Dear Madam, your unworthy friend and servant in Christ.

To Charles Wesley

Madeley, Sept. 9th, 1763

My Dear Sir—I see that we ought to learn continually to cast our burdens on the Lord, who alone can bear them without fatigue and pain. If M—— returns, the Lord may correct his errors, and give him so to insist on the fruits of faith as to prevent antinomianism. I believe him sincere; and though obstinate and suspicious, I am persuaded he has a true desire to know the will and live the life of God. I reply in the same words you quoted to me in one of your letters, "Don't be afraid of a wreck, for Jesus is in the ship." After the most violent storm, the Lord will, perhaps, all at once bring our ship into the desired haven.

You ask me a very singular question with respect to women. I shall, however, answer it with a smile, as I suppose you asked it. You might have remarked that for some days before I set off for Madeley, I considered matrimony with a different eye to what I had done: and the person who then presented herself to my imagination was Miss Bosanquet. Her image pursued me for some hours the last day, and that so warmly that I should, perhaps, have lost my peace, if a suspicion of the truth of Juvenal's proverb, "*Veniunt a dote fagittae*," had not made me blush, fight, and fly to Jesus, Who delivered me at the same moment from her image and the idea of marriage. Since that time I have been more than ever on my guard against admitting the idea of matrimony, sometimes by the consideration of the love of Jesus, which ought to be my whole felicity, and at others by the following reflections.

It is true the Scripture says that a good wife is a gift of the Lord, and it is also true that there may be one in a thousand; but who would put in a lottery where are 999 blanks to one prize? And suppose I could discover this Phoenix, this woman of a thousand, what should I gain by it? A distressing refusal. How could she choose such a man as me? If, notwithstanding all my self love, I am compelled cordially to despise myself, could I be so wanting in generosity as to expect another to do that for me which I cannot do for myself—to engage to love, to esteem, and to honor me?

I will throw on my paper some reflections which the last paragraph of your letter gave rise to, and I beg you will weigh them with me in the balances of the sanctuary.

Reasons for and against Matrimony

For:

(1) A tender friendship is, after the love of Christ, the greatest felicity of life; and a happy marriage is nothing but such a friendship between two persons of different sexes.

(2) A wife might deliver me from the difficulties of housekeeping, etc.

(3) Some objections and scandals may be avoided by marriage.

(4) A pious and zealous wife might be as useful as myself; nay, she might be much more so among my female parishioners, who greatly need an inspectress.

Against:

(1) Death will shortly end all particular friendships. The happier the state of marriage, the more afflicting is widowhood. Besides, we may try a friend and reject him after trial, but we can't know a wife till it is too late to part with her.

(2) Marriage brings after it an hundred cares and expenses—children, a family, etc.

(3) If matrimony is not happy, it is the most fertile source of scandals.

(4) I have 1000 to 1 to fear that a wife instead of being a help may be indolent, and consequently useless; or humorsome, haughty, capricious, and consequently a heavy curse.

TO MR. VAUGHAN

DEAR SIR—As you desire me to tell you simply what I think of the state of your soul as described in your letter, I will do it as the Lord shall enable me.

I praise Him that He has begun a good work in you, which I make no doubt He will finish if you do not counteract the operations of His grace. Your having sometimes free access to the Throne of Grace, but soon falling back into deadness and darkness, is the common experience of many who walk sincerely, though slowly, towards Sion. It argues, on one side, the drawings of faith; and on the other, the power of unbelief. I would compare such souls to the child of the Patriarch, who came to the birth, nay, saw the light of this world, and yet returned again into his mother's womb, until, after a greater struggle, he broke through all that was in his way, and left the place where he had been so long in prison.

If you fall short, be not cast down. On the contrary, rejoice that God has begun and will finish His work in you. Strive more earnestly to enter in at the strait gate. Watch more unto prayer, and pray for that faith which enables the believer *now* to lay hold on eternal life. Remember, however, that your prayers will not avail much unless you deny yourself and take up every cross which the Lord suffers men, devils, or your own heart to lay upon you. In the name of Jesus, and in the power of His might, break through all; and you will find daily more and more that Jesus is the light of the world, and that he who follows Him shall not walk in darkness. The peace of Jesus be with you. Farewell.

TO MISS HATTON

Madeley, March 5, 1764

DEAR MADAM—You seem not to have a clear idea of the happiness of the love of Jesus, or, at least, of your privilege of loving Him again. Your dullness in private prayer arises from the want of familiar friendship with Jesus. To obviate it, go to your closet as if you were going to meet the dearest friend you ever had. Cast yourself immediately at His feet, bemoan your coldness before Him, extol His love to you until your heart breaks with a desire to love Him, yea, till it actually melts with His love. Be you, if not the importunate widow, at least the importunate virgin. Get your Lord to avenge you of your adversary—I mean your *cold heart.*

You ask from me some directions to get a *mortified* spirit. To get this, get recollection. Recollection is a dwelling within ourselves—being abstracted from the creature and turned towards God. It is both outward and inward.

Outward recollection consists in silence from all idle and superfluous words, and a wise disentanglement from the world, keeping to our own business, observing and following the order of God for ourselves, and shutting the ear against all curious and unprofitable matters.

Inward recollection consists in shutting the door of the senses, a deep attention to the presence of God, and a continual care of entertaining holy thoughts for fear of spiritual idleness. Through the power of the Spirit, let this recollection be steady even in the midst of hurrying business. Let it be calm and peaceable. Let it be lasting. "Watch and pray, lest ye enter into temptation."

To maintain this recollection, beware of engaging too deeply—beyond what is necessary—in outward things. Beware of suffering your affections to be entangled by worldly vanities, your imagination to amuse itself with unprofitable objects, and of indulging yourself in the commission of what are called "small faults."

For want of continuing in a recollected frame all the day, our times of prayer are frequently dry and useless. Imagination prevails and the heart wanders, whereas we pass easily from recollection to delightful prayer. Without this spirit, there can be no useful self-denial, nor can we know ourselves. Where it dwells, however, it makes the soul all eye, all ear; it traces and discovers sin, repels its first assaults, or crushes it in its earliest risings.

In recollection let your mind act according to the drawings of grace. It will probably lead you either to contemplate Jesus as crucified and interceding for you, etc., or to watch your senses and suppress your passions, to keep before God in respectful silence of heart, and to watch and follow the motions of grace and feed on the promises.

But take care here to be more taken up with the thoughts of God than of yourself. Consider how hardly recollection is sometimes obtained; how easily it is lost. Use no forced labor to raise a particular frame. Do not tire, fret, and grow impatient if you have no comfort, but meekly acquiesce and confess yourself unworthy of it. Lie prostrate in humble submission before God, and patiently wait for the smiles of Jesus.

May the following motives stir you up to the pursuit of recollection. (1) We must forsake all and die to all first by recollection. (2) Without it, God's voice cannot be heard in the soul. (3) It is the altar on which we must offer up our Isaacs. (4) It is instrumentally a ladder (if I may be allowed the expression) to descend into God. (5) By it the soul gets to its center, out of which it cannot rest. (6) Man's soul is the temple of God—recollection the *holy of holies*. (7) As the wicked by recollection find hell in their hearts, so faithful souls find Heaven. (8) Without recollection all means of grace are useless or make but a light and transitory impression.

If we would be recollected, we must expect to suffer. Sometimes God does not speak immediately to the heart; we must then continue to listen with a more humble silence. Sometimes assaults of the heart or of the temper may follow, together with weariness and a desire to turn the mind to something else. Here we must be patient; by patience unwearied we inherit the promises.

Dissipated souls are severely punished. If any man abide not in Christ, he is cast out as a branch—cast out of the light of God's countenance—and barrenness follows in the use of the means. The world and Satan gather and use him for their service. He is cast into the fire of the passions, guilt, temptation, and perhaps hell.

As dissipation always meets its punishment, so recollection never fails of its reward. After a patient waiting comes communion with God and the sweet sense of His peace and love. Recollection is a castle, an inviolable fortress against the world and the Devil. It renders all times and places alike, and is the habitation where Christ and His Bride dwell.

I give you these hints, not to set Christ aside, but that you may, according to the light and power given to you, take these stones and place them upon the chief corner stone and cement them with the blood of Jesus, until the superstructure, in some measure, answers to the excellence of the foundation. I beg an interest in your prayers for myself and those committed to my charge, and am, with sincerity, Madam, your servant for Christ's sake.

To Miss Hatton

Madeley, Sept. 3rd, 1764

Dear Madam—I think the state your soul is in is not uncommon. The only advice I can at present give you is not to look at self, except it be to believe it away. Be generously determined not to live easy, without the thought of Jesus on your mind, and His love, or at least endeavors after it, in your heart. Then get that love, or the increase of it, by obstinately believing the love of Christ to you, till you are shamed into some return of it. A passage I have found much relief from when my soul has been in the state you describe is: "Likewise reckon ye also yourselves to be dead indeed unto sin, but alive unto God through Jesus Christ our Lord" (Rom. 6:11). This reckoning by faith, I find, is not reckoning without one's host; but Christ is always ready to set His hand to the bill which faith draws.

With respect to the hindrances your worldly business lays in the way of your soul, I would have you to be persuaded that they are by no means insurmountable. The following means, in due subordination to faith in Jesus, may, by the blessing of God, be of service to you.

(1) Get up early and save time, before you go to business, to put on the whole armor of God by close meditation and earnest prayer.

(2) Consider the temptation that most easily besets you, whether it be hurry, vanity, lightness, or want of recollection to do what you do as unto God. Ponder the consequences of those sins, see your weakness to resist them, and endeavor to obtain a more feeling sense of your helplessness. When you have this, you will naturally watch unto prayer and look to Christ for strength from moment to moment.

(3) When your mind hath been drawn aside, do not fret or let yourself go down the stream of nature, as if it were in vain to attempt to swim against it; but confess your fault and calmly resume your former endeavor with more humility and watchfulness.

(4) Steal from business now and then, though for two or three minutes only, and in the corner where you can be least observed pour out your soul in confession, or a short ejaculation at the feet of Jesus for power to watch and to believe that He can keep you watching. May you feelingly believe that He hath bought the power for you, and then of a truth you will find it done to you according to your faith… I am, etc.

To Miss Hatton

Madeley, Dec., 1764

Dear Madam—I am sensible how much I need advice in a thousand particulars, and how incapable I am safely to direct anyone. I shall, nevertheless, venture to throw upon this sheet the following observations as they came to my mind on the reading of your letter.

You cannot expect on the Gospel plan to attain to such a carriage as will please all with whom you converse. The Son of God, the original of all human perfection, was blamed sometimes for His silence, and sometimes for His speaking, etc., and shall the handmaid be above her Master?

There is no sin in wearing such things as you have by you, if they are not out of character—I mean if they are necessary for your station and characterize your rank.

There is no sin in allowing yourself a little more latitude of speech, provided you listen to Christ by inward attention to His teaching, and the end of what you say may be to introduce what is useful and edifying; for God judgeth of words according to the intention of the speaker. I may speak idly even in the pulpit; and I may speak to edification in the market if what I say is either necessary, or proper to introduce, or drive the nail of a profitable truth. Some parables of our Lord would have been deemed idle talk had it not been for the end He pursued, and, upon the whole, accomplished by them. No particular rule can be given here. A thousand circumstances of persons, tempers, places, times, states, etc., will necessarily vary a Christian's plan.

There is no sin in looking cheerful. No, it is our duty to be cheerful—"Rejoice evermore." And if it is our duty always to be filled with joy, it is our duty to appear what we are in reality. I hope, however, your friends know how to distinguish between cheerfulness and levity.

If you want to recommend religion to those you converse with and, in many instances, to pluck up offence by the root, let your heart lie where Mary's body did. Keep close to Jesus. Be attentive to His still, small voice, and He will fill you with humble love, and such love will teach you, without any rule, as by the instinct of your new nature, to become "all things to all men."

You ask what the apostle means by that expression. It is certain he did not mean to overset his own precept, "Be not conformed to the world." I apprehend that in every case wherein we might promote the spiritual or temporal good of any one by doing or suffering things of an indifferent nature, or even painful and disagreeable to us, we ought to be ready to become all things to all—provided the good we propose is superior to the inconveniences to which we submit. Here also we stand in need of humble love and meek wisdom, that we may so weigh circumstances as to form a right judgment in all things.

I am glad the Lord strips you. I wish *self* may never clothe you again. Beware of stiff singularity in things *barely indifferent*—it is self in disguise. And it is so much the more dangerous as it comes recommended by a serious, self denying, religious appearance.

I hope the shortcomings of some about you will not prevent your eying the prize of a glorious conformity to our blessed Head. It is to be feared that not a few of those who talk of having attained it have mistaken the way; they are still something, and I apprehend an important step towards that conformity is to become nothing, or rather with St. Paul to become in our own eyes the chief of sinners and the least of saints.

Mr. Harris seems to me one among ten thousand. He has left a peculiar blessing behind him in this place. The God of peace give us all the blessings that the Messenger and the Mediator of the New Covenant brought with Him, at this time, into the world. May we so receive Him that by a blessed exchange as He is clad with our flesh, so we may put on Him and be covered with His righteousness and filled with His Spirit! Salute the Church in your house. From your servant in the Gospel.

To Miss Hatton

Madeley, Jan. 31st, 1765

Dear Madam—"You strive, pray, resist, but are little the better." Yet pray, strive, and resist on. It is good to be tried and to get a blessing in the very fire. We shall then know how to value it properly. But let me be free with you, Madam. Do you pray, resist, and strive against wanderings with any *steadiness*? And do you do it in *cheerful hope* to overcome through the blood of the Lamb? When you have been unhinged from Christ, in mind or heart, do you with stronger indignation against wanderings, a calmer expectation of the assistance of the Spirit, and a deeper agony of faith, seek to be avenged of your Adversary? Do you imitate the importunate widow? If this be the case, you will not complain long; for whatsoever we thus ask in the name of Christ, we shall surely receive. And should the Lord, for reasons best known to Himself, try your faith and hope, yet that longer trial will be found to praise and honor in the end. Only faint not, and when you find yourself inclined to do so, in all haste fly to the cordial of the promises, and determine to take nothing else till your heart is revived and made strong again.

The same power of God, through praying faith, is necessary to keep you from reasoning unprofitably. Whenever this arises to any height, there is one thing wanting—a steadily exerted will never thus to reason. We cannot be so easily betrayed or slide away into this snare of the devil so easily as into the other. I apprehend that whosoever abides steadily purposed not to reason, shall not do it. The will starts aside first, the resolution of course follows, and the tempter easily takes their place. Get willing, truly willing under the cross, and keep there to keep your will, or you will beat the air.

Last Sunday I preached two sermons upon Heb. 11:1. I see so much in that faith of the apostle that I can hardly pray for anything besides that evidence of things not seen, that substance of things hoped for. To how many mistakes and fatal errors have we opened the door by varying from the apostle and pretending to be wiser than the Holy Ghost! The Lord fill you and yours with that faith! Farewell.

To Miss Hatton

Madeley, June 2nd, 1765

Dear Madam—I thank you for the letter of your correspondent. What he says about luminous joy may sometimes be the case in some of God's dear children. But I apprehend that God's design in withholding from them those gracious influences which work upon and melt the sensitive, affectionate part in the soul, is to put us more upon using the nobler powers—the *understanding* and the *will*. These are always more in the reach of a child of God, while the other greatly depend upon the texture of the animal frame. And if they are not stirred in a natural way, the Spirit of God can alone, without our concurrence in general, excite them. Therefore believe, love, take up your cross, and run after Jesus.

You must let friends and foes talk about your dress, while you mind only Jesus, His Word, and your own conscience. You talk of hearing me soon. I dare never invite anyone to hear *me*, though I am glad to see my friends. But now I can invite you with pleasure to come and hear a preacher who, under God, will make you amends for the trouble of a journey to Madeley. His name is M———. He may possibly stay a Sunday or two more with me. But Jesus has promised to be always with His poor followers. To His merciful hand I commend both you and your unworthy friend.

To Alexander Mather

My Dear Brother—… I desire you will call at the Bank as often as you have opportunity. An occasional exhortation from you or your fellow-laborer at the Bank, Dale, etc. will be esteemed a favor. I hope that my stepping, as Providence directs, to any of your places (leaving to you the management of the Societies) will be deemed no encroachment. In short, we need not make *two parties*. I know but one Heaven below, and that is Jesus's love. Let us both go and abide in it, and when we have gathered as many as we can to go with us, too many will still stay behind.

I find there are in the ministry, as in the common experience of Christians, times which may be compared to Winter: no great stir is made in the world of grace beside that of storms and offenses, and the growth of the trees of the Lord is not showy. But when the tender buds of brotherly and redeeming love begin to fill, Spring is at hand. The Lord give us harvest after seed time! Let us wait for fruit as the husbandman, and remember that he who believes does not make haste. The love of Christ be with us all! Pray for me.

To His Congregation

Bath, October 30, 1765

To those that love the Lord Jesus Christ in and about Madeley: Peace be multiplied to you from God the Father, and from our Lord Jesus Christ, through the operations of the Holy Ghost. Amen.

By the help of divine Providence and the assistance of your prayers I came safe here. I was, and am still, a good deal weighed down under the sense of my own insufficiency to preach the unsearchable riches of Christ to poor, dying souls.

This place is the seat of Satan's gaudy throne. The Lord hath, nevertheless, a few names here who are not ashamed of Him, and of whom He is not ashamed, both among the poor and among the rich. There are not many of the last, though blessed be God for any one. It is a great miracle if one camel passes through the eye of a needle, or in other words, if one rich man enters into the Kingdom of Heaven. I thank God that none of you are rich in the things of this world. You are freed from a double snare, even from Dives' portion in this life. May you know the happiness attending your state! It is a mercy to be driven to the Throne of Grace even by bodily want, and to live in dependence on divine mercy for a morsel of bread.

I have been sowing the seed the Lord hath given me both in Bath and Bristol. I hope your prayers have not been lost upon me as a minister, for though I have not been enabled to discharge my office as I would, the Lord hath yet, in some measure, stood by me and overruled my foolishness and helplessness. I am much supported by the thought that you bear me on your hearts; and when you come to the Throne of Grace to ask a blessing for me in the name of Jesus, the Lord doth in no wise cast you out.

In regard to the state of my soul, I find, blessed be God, that as my day is, so is my strength to travel on, either through good or bad report. My absence from you answers two good ends to me: First, I feel more my insufficiency and the need of being daily ordained by Christ to preach His Gospel. Secondly, I shall value the more my privileges among you, please God I return safely to you. I had yesterday a most advantageous offer made me of going, free of cost, to visit my mother, brothers, and sisters in the flesh, whom I have not seen for eighteen years. However, I find my relations in the spirit nearer and dearer to me than my relations in the flesh. I have, therefore, rejected the kind offer, that I may return among you and be comforted by the mutual faith both of you and me.

I hope, dear brethren, you improve much under the ministry of that faithful servant of God, Mr. Brown, whom Providence blesses you with. Make haste to gather the honey of knowledge and grace as it drops from his lips; and may I find the hive of your hearts so full of it on my return that I may share with you in the heavenly store. In order to this, beseech the Lord to excite your hunger and thirst for Jesus's flesh and blood and to increase your desire of the sincere milk of the Word. When people are hungry, they will find time for their meals; a good appetite does not think a meal a day too much. As you go to your spiritual meals, do not forget to pray all the way and to feast your souls in hopes of hearing some good news from Heaven, and from Jesus, the faithful, loving Friend Whom you have there. When you return, be sure to carry the unsearchable riches of Jesus' dying and rising love home to your houses in the vessel of a believing heart.

Let your light be attended with the warmth of love. Be not satisfied to know the way to Heaven, but walk in it immediately, constantly, and joyfully. Be all truly in earnest. You may, indeed, impose upon your brethren by a formal attendance on the means of grace, but you cannot deceive the Searcher of hearts. Let Him always see your hearts struggling towards Him; and if you fall through heaviness, sloth, or unbelief, do not make a bad matter worse by continuing helpless in the ditch of sin and guilt. Up, and away to the fountain of Jesus's blood. It will not only wash away the guilt of past sins, but strengthen you to tread all iniquity under your feet for the time to come. Never forget that the soul of the diligent shall be made fat. The Lord will spue the lukewarm out of His mouth unless He gets that love which makes a person fervent in spirit, diligent in business, serving the Lord.

You know the way to get this love is, (1) To consider the free mercy of God and to believe in the pardoning love of Jesus, Who died, the Just for the unjust, to bring us to God. (2) To be frequently, if not constantly, applying this faith with all the attention of your mind and all the fervor of your heart. "Lord, I am lost, but Christ hath died." (3) To try actually to love, as you can, by setting your affections on Christ, Whom you see not; and for His sake, on your brethren whom you do see. (4) To use much private prayer for yourselves and others, and to try to keep up that communion with God and your absent brethren. I beg in order to this that you will not forsake the assembling of yourselves together, as the manner of some is. When you meet as a society, be neither backward nor forward to speak. Esteem yourselves every one as the meanest in company, and be glad to sit at the feet of the lowest. If you are tempted against any one, yield not to the temptation. Pray much for that love which hopes all things and puts the best construction even upon the worst of failings.

I beg for Christ's sake that I may find no divisions nor offenses among you on my return. "If there be… any consolation in Christ, if any comfort of love, if any fellowship of the Spirit, if any bowels and mercies, fulfill ye my joy, that ye be like-minded, having the same love, being of one accord, of one mind. Let nothing be done through strife or vainglory; but in lowliness of mind let each esteem other better than themselves."

I earnestly request the continuance of your prayers for me, both as a minister and as your companion in tribulation. Ask particularly that the Lord would keep me from hurting His cause in these parts; and that when Providence shall bring me back among you, I may be more thoroughly furnished for every good work. Pardon me if I do not salute you all by name. My heart does it, if my pen does not. That the blessing of God in Jesus Christ may crown all your hearts and all your meetings is the earnest prayer of, my very dear brethren, Yours, etc., J. F.

To Miss Hatton

Madeley, Jan. 13th, 1766

DEAR MADAM—I am almost ashamed of answering your letters after my long delays, but better late than never. I hope your indulgence will put the best construction upon what time does not allow me to make an apology for.

I do not wonder if ——— etc. hath been a snare to entangle your thoughts, but it is now over; what is that to thee? Follow thou Christ. You may, however, learn this lesson, that the minding Christ and our own souls, with Mary, while we leave the world to Martha, is no easy thing in a day of temptation. No one knows what he is until he is tried, and tried in the tenderest points—love, liberty, esteem, and sharp bodily pain. Lord prepare us for such trials, and may we encounter them in the *whole* armor of God!

This evening I have buried one of the warmest opposers of my ministry, a stout, strong young man aged twenty-four years. About three months ago he came to the church yard with a corpse, but refused to come into the church. When the burial was over, I went to him, and mildly expostulated with him. His constant answer was that he had bound himself never to come to church while I was there, adding that he would take the consequences, etc. Seeing I got nothing, I left him, saying with uncommon warmth (though as far as I can remember without the least touch of resentment), "I am clear of your blood. Henceforth it is upon your own head. You will not come to church upon your legs, prepare to come upon your neighbors' shoulders." He wasted from that time, and to my great surprise hath been buried on the spot where we were when the conversation passed between us. When I visited him in his sickness, he seemed tame as a wolf in a trap. O may God have turned him into a sheep in his last hours!

This last year is the worst I have had here—barren in convictions, fruitful in backslidings. May this prove for us, and for you, the acceptable year of the Lord. I beg your prayers on this behalf.

I have filled my page, but not with Jesus' name. Let your heart contain what my letter lacks—Jesus and His precious blood—Jesus and His free, glorious salvation. Live to Him, breathe for Him. Buy, sell, eat, drink, read, write for Him. Receive Him as yours altogether, and give him your *whole* self, with all that is around you. Take us all, Lord, into Thy gracious favor; stamp us with Thy glorious image, and conduct us to Thy eternal Kingdom!

Present my Christian respects to Mrs. Hatton, your sister, and all your friends, and accept the same from your unworthy brother.

To Miss Hatton

Madeley, May, 1766

My Dear Friend—I am sorry, after the manner of men, that you are ill, but glad in the Spirit that the will of God takes place in you, and that He purges you, that you may bring forth more fruit. Now is the time for you to begin to be a Christian in good earnest—I mean, to follow the Man of Sorrows; and to do it as a lamb who goes to the slaughter and opens not his mouth by way of complaint; though as a Christian, I apprehend you may and ought to open it by way of praise.

One advice I will venture to give you, or rather to transcribe for you out of Isaiah: The believer does not make haste to doubt, to hurry, to forecast, and to reason after the manner of men—"If I am a child of God, why am I not thus and thus?" Let Christ, either suffering for you or ordering your sufferings, be so eyed that you may in a manner forget and lose yourself in Him. Or if a weak and pained body makes you think of wretched self, let it be to lay it down with composure at Jesus' feet, or to take up the burden of the cross with cheerful resignation. I hope to hear soon of your being recovered in body and strengthened in soul by this affliction.

"Is any prayer acceptable to God, which is not the dictates of His own Spirit?" If you mean by the "dictates of the Spirit" His influence on the mind to show us our needs, and upon the heart to make us desire a supply of them, I answer, No. This is because a prayer which hath not at least the above mentioned qualities is only a vain babbling.

"Does a believer always pray with the Spirit's assistance?" Yes, when he prays *as a believer* and not as a parrot; for even at his lowest times he has, more or less, a sight of his needs and a desire to have them supplied. This he could not have, did not the Spirit work upon his mind and heart.

I hope you sink inwardly into nothing, and through nothing into the immensity of God. I see a little, through mercy, into the beauty of humiliation. I find the ministry of condemnation glorious; and I love to take, every moment, the curse out of Moses' hand as well as the blessing out of Christ's. The Lord grant that you and I and all our friends may do it more feelingly and constantly every hour!

May the Physician of soul and body refresh, strengthen, establish, and thoroughly heal you by the virtue of His blood and the word of His power! Bear well, and farewell. Your unworthy servant.

To Miss Hatton

Madeley, May 27, 1766

My Dear Friend—I am glad to hear that the God of all mercy and grace has raised you from the bed of sickness where His *love* had confined you. It is good to see His works in the deep, and then to come and sing His praises in the land of the living. A touch of pain or sickness I find always profitable to me, as it rivets on my soul the thoughts of my nothingness, helplessness, and mortality. It shows me in a clearer light the vanity of all the transitory scenes of life. May your afflictions have the same effect upon you as long as you live. May you be more steadfast than I am to retain the deep impressions which God's gracious rod may have left upon your soul. And may you learn to lay yourself out more for the Lord, and to do whatsoever your hand findeth to do, with all your might, knowing that there is no wisdom nor device in the grave whither we are going.

If a sparrow falleth not to the ground, nor a hair from our head, without our heavenly Father's leave, it is certain that higher circumstances of our life are planned by the wise and gracious Governor of all things. This kind of faith in Providence I find of indispensable necessity to go calmly through life, and I think through death also.

The coming of Mr. Wesley's preachers into my parish gives me no *uneasiness*. As I am sensible that everybody does better, and of course is more acceptable than myself, I should be sorry to deprive any one of a blessing. I rejoice that the work of God goes on by any instrument or in any place…

I fear I have left as great a stink at Bath as Mr. Brown a sweet savor here. Everything is good to me that shows me my unprofitableness more and more. But I desire to grieve that the good of my private humiliation is so much over balanced by the loss of many about me.

The Lord fill you with all peace and joy in your soul, and with all strength and health in your body! My respects wait upon your mother and sister, and all friends. Farewell.

To Miss Hatton

Madeley, June 21, 1766

My Dear Friend—I am much concerned to hear, by Mrs. Power, that you are so weak. But my concern has greatly increased since I was told that the foundation of your illness was laid at Madeley; and I am afraid it was by my imprudence in taking you to the woman with whom we received the sacrament. I ask God's pardon and yours for it, and I hope it will be a means of humbling me and making me more tender of my friends…

You know that I perceived your bodily weakness when you were here, and charged you with what you charge me with, "a neglect of your body." If I was right, I hope you will follow yourself the advice you give me—I am sure you will—the burnt child will dread the fire for the time to come…

Offer yourself to God for life or death, for ease or pain, for strength or weakness. Let Him choose and refuse for you. Only do you choose Him for your present and eternal portion. I want you to be a little bolder in venturing upon the bosom of our Lord. We lose (I for one) much sweetness and many degrees of holiness in being shy of the Friend, the *loving* Friend of sinners. Pray, for God's sake don't forget that your Physician is your *Husband.* The *joy* of the Lord as well as His *peace*, is to be your strength. Love is a passion that needs to be stirred. Do it in all calmness. "I will love Him. I do love Him a little; I shall love Him much, because He has first loved me, etc." Ply, I pray you, this sweet Gospel talk. Accustom yourself to look upon your body as the temple of the Holy Ghost, and meet Him in your heart by simple recollection and a steady belief of these Gospel truths: "He is here," "He is in me," etc. And do not let them go for anything you do feel or do not feel. May God bless, comfort, establish, and raise you! Farewell.

To Miss Ireland

Madeley, July, 1766

My Very Dear Friend—The poor account your father has brought us of your health, and his apprehensions of not seeing you any more before that solemn day when all people, nations, and tongues shall stand together at the bar of God, make me venture (together with my love to you) to send you a few lines. My earnest prayer to God is that they may be blessed to your soul.

First, then, my dear friend, let me beseech you not to flatter yourself with the hopes of living long here on earth. These hopes fill us with worldly thoughts, and make us backward to prepare for our change. I would not, for the world, entertain such thoughts about myself. I have now in my parish a young man who has been these two years under the surgeon's hand. Since they have given him up, which is about two months ago, he has fled to the Lord and found in Him that saving health which surpasses a thousand times that which the surgeons flattered him with. And now he longs to depart and be with Christ which is far better. To see the bridge of life cut off behind us, and to have done with all the thoughts of repairing it to go back into the world, has a natural tendency to make us venture forward to the foot of the cross.

Secondly, my dear, consider how good the Lord is to call you to be transplanted into a better world before you have taken deeper root in this sinful world; and if it is hard to nature to die *now*, how much harder do you think it would be if you lived to be the mother of a family and to cleave to earth by the ties of many new relations, schemes of gain, or prospects of happiness?

Thirdly, reflect on this, that by your illness the Lord, Who forecasts for us, intimates that long life would not be for His glory nor your happiness. I believe He takes many young people from the evil to come and out of the way of those temptations or misfortunes which would have made them miserable in time and in eternity.

Fourthly: your earthly father loves you much—witness the hundreds of miles he has gone for the bare prospect of your health. But, my dear, your heavenly Father loves you a thousand times better; and He is all wisdom as well as all goodness. Allow, then, such a loving, gracious Father to choose for you; and if He chooses death, acquiesce, and say, as you can, "Good is the will of the Lord; His choice must be best!"

Fifthly. Weigh the sinfulness of sin, both original and actual, and firmly believe the wages of sin is death. This will make you patiently accept the punishment, especially if you consider that Jesus Christ, by dying for us, has taken away the sting of death and turned the grave into a passage to a blessed eternity.

Sixthly. Try, my dear, to get nearer to the dear Redeemer. "He hath delivered us from the curse of the law, being made a curse for us" (Gal. 3:13). He hath quenched the wrath of God in His atoning blood. By His atoning blood, by His harmless life and painful death, He has satisfied all the demands of the law and justice of God. By His resurrection He asserted the full discharge of all our spiritual debts. By His ascension into Heaven, where He is gone to prepare us a place, He has opened a way to endless glory. By His powerful intercession and the merits of His blood, which plead continually for us, He keeps that way open. And to encourage us, He assures us that He is "the way, the truth, and the life," and that "he who comes to Him He will in no wise cast out." He mildly offers rest to the heavy laden, pardon to the guilty, strength to the feeble, and life to the dead. You know His words: "I am the resurrection and the life: he that believeth on Me, though he were dead, yet shall he live: and he that liveth and believeth in Me shall never die."

Seventhly. When you have considered your lost estate as a sinner by nature, together with the greatness, the fullness, the freeness, and suitableness of Christ's salvation, and when you have diligently viewed the glories and charms of His person, believe in Him. Without any ceremony, choose Him for your Physician, your Husband, and your King. Be not afraid to venture upon and trust in Him. Cast yourself on Him in frequent acts of reliance, and stay your soul on Him by means of His promises. Pray much for faith, and be not afraid of accepting, using, and thanking God for a *little*. The smoking flax He will not quench. Only pray hard that He would blow it up into a blaze of light and love.

Eighthly. Beware of impatience, repining, and peevishness, which are the sins of sick people. Be gentle, easy to be pleased, and resigned as the bleeding Lamb of God. Wrong tempers indulged grieve, if they do not quench, the Spirit.

Ninthly. Do not repine at being in a strange country, far from your friends; for if your going to France does not answer the end proposed to your body, it will answer a spiritual end to your soul. God suffers the broken reeds of your acquaintance to be out of your reach so that you may not catch at them, and that you may, at once, cast your lonesome soul on the bosom of Him Who fills Heaven and earth.

Tenthly. In praying, reading, hearing any person read, and meditating, do not consult feeble, fainting, weary flesh and blood; for at this rate death may find you idle and supine instead of striving to enter in at the strait gate. And when your spirits and vigor fail, remember that the Lord is the strength of your life, and your portion for ever. O death, where is thy sting? Thanks be to God, Who giveth us the victory, through Jesus Christ our Lord!

Many pray hard for you that you may acquit yourself living or dying, in ease or in pain, as a wise virgin and as a good soldier of Jesus Christ. But above all, Jesus, the Captain of your salvation, and the High Priest of your profession, intercedes mightily for you. Look to Him and be saved, even from the ends of France. To His pity, love, and power I recommend you. May He bless you, my dear friend—lift up the light of His countenance upon you, and give you peace and courage, repentance, faith, hope, and patient love, both now and evermore! I am your affectionate, sincere friend and servant in Jesus.

To James Ireland

Madeley, July, 1766

My Very Dear Friend—Your absence made me postpone thanking you for all the kindness you showed me when at Bristol. And to lay me under still greater obligation, you have sent me a hamper full of wine and broad cloth—as if it were not enough to adorn and cover the outside, but you must also warm and nourish the inside of the body! To this you have added a kind but melancholy letter from Dover. Melancholy, I say, as well as kind, by the account it gives of the worldliness of our Protestant brethren abroad, and of the little hope you have of seeing your daughter again…

I submit to be clothed and nourished by you, as your servants are, without having the happiness of serving you. To yield to this is as hard to friendship as to submit to be saved by free grace without one scrap of our own righteousness. However, we are allowed, both in religion and friendship, to ease ourselves by thanks and prayers till we have an opportunity of doing it by actions.

I thank you, then, my dear friend, and pray to God that you may receive His benefits as I do yours! Your broad cloth can lap me round two or three times; but the mantle of Jesus' righteousness can cover your soul a thousand times. The cloth, fine and good as it is, will not keep out a hard shower; but that garment of salvation will keep out even a shower of brimstone and fire. Your cloth will wear out, but that fine linen, the righteousness of the saints, will appear with a finer luster the more it is worn. The moth may fret your present, or the tailor may spoil it in cutting; but the present which Jesus has made you is out of the reach of the spoiler and ready for present wear. Nor is there any fear of cutting it out wrong, for it is seamless, woven from the top throughout, with the white unbroken warp of thirty-three years perfect obedience, and the red weft of His agony and sufferings unto death.

Now, my dear friend, let me beseech you to accept of this heavenly present as I accept of your earthly one. I did not send you one farthing to purchase it; it came unsought, unasked, unexpected, as the Seed of the woman; and it came just as I was sending a tailor to buy me some cloth for a new coat. Immediately I stopped him, and I hope that when you next see me, it will be in your present. Now let Jesus see you in His. Walk in white, adorn His Gospel, while He beautifies you with the garment of salvation. Accept it freely. Wear no more the old rusty coat of nature and self-righteousness. Send no more to have it patched. Make your boast of an unbought suit, and love to wear the livery of Jesus. You will then love to do His work; it will be your meat and drink to do it. And in order that you may be vigorous in doing it, as I shall take a little of your wine for my stomach's sake, take you a good deal of the wine of the Kingdom for your soul's sake. Every promise of the Gospel is a bottle, a cask that has a spring within, and can never be drawn out. But draw the cork of unbelief, and drink abundantly, O beloved, nor be afraid of intoxication; and if an inflammation follows, it will only be that of divine love.

I beg you will be more free with the heavenly wine than I have been with the earthly, which you sent me. I have not tasted it yet, but whose fault is it? Not yours certainly, but mine. If you do not drink daily spiritual health and vigor out of the cup of salvation, whose fault is it? Not Jesus', but yours! For He gives you His righteousness to cover your nakedness, and the consolations of His Spirit to cheer and invigorate your soul. Accept and use. Wear, drink, and live to God. That you may heartily and constantly do this is my sincere prayer for you and yours—especially your poor daughter, whom I trust you have resigned into the hands of Him to Whom she is nearer than to you. The wise Disposer of all things knows what is best for her. The hairs of her head, much more the days of her life, are all numbered. The Lord often destroys the body that the soul may be saved. And if this is the case here, as one may reasonably hope, you will not say unto the Lord, "What doest Thou?" But say with the father who lost two sons in one day, "It is the Lord, let Him do whatsoever He pleaseth," or with him who lost ten children at one stroke, "The Lord gave, and the Lord taketh away, and blessed be the name of the Lord!" Adieu.

To Miss Hatton

Madeley, July 30th, 1766

My Dear Friend—So you are likely to be at rest first! Well, the Lord's will be done. I should be glad to have you stay to help us to the Kingdom of God; but if God wants to take you there, and house you before a storm, I shall only cry, "One of the chariots of Israel and the horsemen thereof," and try to make the best of my way after you.

A calm receiving of the Gospel tidings, upon a conviction of your lost estate, with suitable tempers, is a sign that you are in a *safe state*; but I want you altogether in a *comfortable* one. Your business, I apprehend, is not to turn the dunghill of nature, but to suck the Gospel milk. Dwell much, if not altogether, upon free justification through the redemption that is in Christ Jesus. View the sufficiency, fullness, suitableness, freeness of His atonement and righteousness; and hide yourself without delay under both. Look at death only as a door to let you out of manifold infirmities and pains, into the arms of Jesus, your heavenly Bridegroom. Stir up faith, hope, and love—that is trimming your lamp.

Since last Monday I find the burden of your soul upon mine in a very particular manner, and I hope that I shall not cease to pray for you, that you may go not only calmly, but joyfully, the way of all flesh. I have got some praying souls to share with me in that profitable work, and I hope you will meet our spirits at the Throne of Grace as we do yours.

Let me have the comfort of thinking that you are with your Physician, Husband, and All, Who will order all things for the best. Pray hard, believe harder, and love hardest. Let the cry of your soul be, "None but Jesus living, none but Jesus dying." Let Christ be your life, and then death, whether it comes sooner or later, will be your gain.

Mr. Glazebrook waits for these lines, and I conclude by again entreating you to believe. "Only believe," said Jesus to the Ruler, and faith will work by love, and love by a desire to depart and to be with Christ. God the Father, Son, and Holy Ghost bless, uphold, and comfort you! Farewell, and forget not to pray for your helpless friend.

To Miss ———

MY VERY DEAR FRIEND— … I beseech you to pray that I may have power to tarry at the footstool of divine mercy for a day of Pentecost, till I am endued with power from on high for the work of the ministry and the blessings of Christianity.

I know not whether I am wrong in this respect, but I expect a power from on high to make me what I am not—an instrument to show forth the praises of the Redeemer, and to do some good to the souls of my fellow creatures. Until this power comes, it appears to me that I spend my paltry strength in vain, and that

I might as well sit still. But I know I must keep rowing though the wind be contrary, till Jesus comes walking upon the waters, though it were in the last watch of the night.

You see that while you praise on the top of the mountain, I hang my untuned harp on the mournful willow at the bottom. But Jesus was in Gethsemane as well as on Tabor, and while He blesses you, He sympathizes with me. But this is speaking too much about self; *good* and *bad* self must be equally denied, and He that is the fullness of Him Who fills all in all must fill my thoughts, my desires, my letters, and my all. Come then, Lord, come and drop into our souls as the dew into Gideon's fleece. Drop Thy blessing on these lines, and may Thy sweet name, Jesus, Emmanuel, God with us, be as ointment and rich perfumes poured upon my dear Sister's soul! Spread Thy wings of love over her. Reward her an hundredfold in temporal and spiritual blessings, for the temporal and spiritual mercies she hath bestowed upon me as Thy servant; and vouchsafe to keep me such!

I want you to write to me what you think of the *life of faith*, and whether you breathe it without interruption; whether you *never* leave that rich palace—Christ—to return to that dungeon—self. What are your feelings when faith is at its lowest ebb, and when it acts most powerfully? I should be glad also if you would answer these questions: What views have you of another world? What sense have you of the nearness of Christ? What degree of fellowship with the souls nearest your heart? What particular intimations of the will of God in intricate affairs and material steps? And whether you can reconcile the *life of faith* with one wrong temper in the heart.

If you are so good as to answer these questions at large, you will oblige me more than if you were to send me 200 waistcoats and as many pairs of stockings. Jesus is life, love, power, truth, and righteousness. Jesus is ours; yea, He is over all, through all, and in us all. May we so fathom this mystery, and so evidence the reality of it, that many may see and fear and turn to the Lord! My kind love and thanks wait upon your sisters, etc. Farewell in Jesus. Pray for your obliged, unworthy servant.

To Miss Hatton

Madeley, Sept., 1766

My Very Dear Friend—God wonderfully supports your tottering clay so that He may fill up what is lacking in your faith. Concur with the merciful design. Arise in spirit, shake off the dust of earthly thoughts, put on your glorious apparel—put on, every moment, the Lord Jesus Christ. Dare to believe—on Christ lay hold. Wrestle with Christ in mighty, or even in feeble, prayer. He breaks not the bruised reed. Let the reed be grafted, by simple faith, in the true vine—in the tree of life—and it will bring forth glorious fruit: not only resignation, but power to welcome the King disarmed of his terrors, and turned into a messenger of joy and a guide, under Christ, to heavenly happiness. Let not one feeble breath pass without carrying an act of desire or of faith towards Christ. Bestir yourself to lay hold on God, and when you find an absolute want of power, be you the more careful to lie at the feet of Him Who hath all power given Him in earth and Heaven *for you.* Farewell, my dear friend, that is, be found in Christ; for there only can we fare well, whether we live or die.

To His Congregation

Oakhall, October 1766

To Those Who Love or Fear the Lord Jesus Christ at Madeley—Grace, peace, and love be multiplied to you from our God and Savior Jesus Christ.

Providence, my dear brethren, called me so suddenly from you that I had not time to take my leave and recommend myself to your prayers. But I hope the good Spirit of our God, which is the Spirit of love and supplication, has brought me to your remembrance as the poorest and weakest of Christ's ministers, and, consequently, as one whose hands stand most in need of being strengthened and lifted up by your prayers. Pray on, then, for yourselves, for one another, and for him whose glory is to minister to you in holy things, and whose sorrow it is not to do it in a manner more suitable to the majesty of the Gospel and more profitable to your souls.

My heart is with you, and yet I bear patiently this bodily separation for three reasons. First, the variety of more faithful and able ministers whom you have during my absence is more likely to be serviceable to you than my presence among you. I would always prefer your profit to my satisfaction. Secondly, I hope Providence will give me those opportunities of conversing and praying with a greater variety of experienced Christians, which will tend to my own improvement, and I trust, in the end, to yours. Thirdly, I flatter myself that after some weeks absence my ministry will be recommended by the advantage of novelty, which, the more the pity, goes farther with some than the Word itself. In the meantime I shall give you some advice which, it may be, will prove both suitable and profitable to you.

1. Endeavor to improve daily under the ministry which Providence blesses you with. Be careful to attend it with diligence, faith, and prayer. Would it not be a great shame if, when ministers come thirty or forty miles to offer you peace, pardon, strength, and comfort in the name of God, any of you should slight the glorious message, or hear it as if it were nothing to you and as if you heard it not? See, then, that you never come from a sermon without being more deeply convinced of sin and of righteousness.

2. Use more prayer before you go to church. Consider that your next appearance there may be in a coffin. Entreat the Lord to give you now so to hunger and thirst after righteousness that you may be filled. Hungry people never go fasting from a feast. Call to mind the text I preached from the last Sunday but one before I left you. "Wherefore, laying aside all malice…" (1 Pet. 2:1).

3. When you are under the Word, beware of sitting as judges rather than as criminals. Many judge of the manner, matter, voice, and person of the preacher. You, perhaps, judge all the congregation, when you should judge yourselves worthy of eternal death,

yet worthy of eternal life through the worthiness of Him Who stood and was condemned at Pilate's bar for you. The moment you have done crying to God as guilty, or thanking Christ as reprieved criminals, you have reason to conclude that this advice is leveled at you.

4. When you have used a means of grace, and do not find yourselves sensibly quickened, let it be a matter of deep humiliation to you. For want of repenting of their unbelief and hardness of heart, some get into a habit of deadness and indolence; and they come to be as insensible and as little ashamed of themselves for it as stones.

5. Beware of the inconsistent behavior of those who complain they are full of wanderings in the evening, under the Word, when they have suffered their minds to wander from Christ all the day long. O! get acquainted with Him, that you may walk in Him and with Him. Whatsoever you do or say, especially in the things of God, do or say it as if Christ were before, behind, and on every side of you. Indeed He is so, whether you consider it or not; for if when He visibly appeared on earth He called Himself "the Son of Man Who is in Heaven," how much more then is He present on earth now that He makes His immediate appearance in Heaven?

Make your conscience maintain a sense of His blessed presence all the day long, and then all the day long you will have a feast. For can you conceive any thing more delightful than to be always at the fountain of love, beauty, and joy—at the spring of power, wisdom, goodness, and truth? Can there be a purer and more melting happiness than to be with the best of fathers, the kindest of brothers, the most generous of benefactors, and the tenderest of husbands? Now Jesus is all this and much more to the believing soul. O! believe, my friends, in Jesus now, through a continual now. And, until you can thus believe, mourn over your unbelieving hearts. Drag them to Him. Think of the efficacy of His blood which was shed for the ungodly, and wait for the spirit of faith from on high.

6. Some of you wonder why you cannot believe—why you cannot see Jesus with the eye of your mind and delight in Him

with all the affections of your heart. I apprehend the reason to be one of these, or, perhaps, all of them.

First, you are not poor, lost, undone, helpless sinners in yourselves. You indulge spiritual and refined self-righteousness. You are not yet dead to the law and quite slain by the commandment. Now the Kingdom of Heaven belongs to none but the poor in spirit. Jesus came to save none but the lost. What wonder, then, if Jesus be nothing to you, and if you do not live in His Kingdom of peace, righteousness, and joy in the Holy Ghost?

Secondly, perhaps you spend your time in curious reasonings, instead of casting yourselves down as forlorn sinners at Christ's feet, leaving it to Him to bless you when, in what manner, and in whatever degree He pleases. Know that He is the wise and sovereign Lord, and that it is your duty to lie before Him as clay—as fools—as sinful nothings.

Thirdly, perhaps some of you willfully keep idols of one kind or other. You indulge some sin against light and knowledge, and it is neither matter of humiliation nor confession to you. The love of praise, of the world, of money, and of sensual gratifications, when not lamented, are as implacable enemies to Christ as Judas and Herod. How can you believe, seeing you seek the honor that cometh of men? Hew, then, your Agags in pieces before the Lord. Run from your Delilahs to Jesus. Cut off the right hand, and pluck out the right eye that offends you. "Come out from among them, and be ye separate, saith the Lord ... and I will receive you."

Nevertheless, when you strive, be careful not to make yourself a righteousness of your strivings. Remember that meritorious, justifying righteousness is finished and brought in; your works can no more add to it than your sins can diminish from it. Shout, then, "the Lord our righteousness." If you feel yourselves undone sinners, humbly, yet boldly say, "In the Lord I have righteousness and strength."

When I was in London, I endeavored to make the most of my time—that is to say, to hear, to receive, and practise the Word. Accordingly I went to Mr. Whitefield's tabernacle and heard him give his society a most excellent exhortation upon love. He began by observing that when the Apostle John was old and past walking and preaching, he would not forsake the assembling himself with the brethren, as the manner of too many is, upon little or no pretense at all. On the contrary, he got himself carried to their meeting, and, with his last thread of voice, preached to them his final sermon, consisting of this one sentence, "My little children, love one another."

I wish, I pray, I earnestly beseech you to follow that evangelical, apostolic advice. Till God make you all little children, little in your own eyes and simple as little children, give me leave to say, my dear brethren, "love one another," and of course, judge not, provoke not, and be not shy one of another. Bear ye one another's burdens, and so fulfill the law of Christ. Bear with one another's infirmities, and do not easily cast off any one, no, not for sin—except it be obstinately persisted in.

My sheet is full, and so is my heart, of good wishes for you and ardent longings after you all. When I return, let me have the comfort of finding you all believing and loving. Farewell, my dear brethren. The blessing of God be with you all! This is the earnest desire of your unworthy minister.

To Miss Hatton

Madeley, Jan. 9th, 1767

My Dear Friend—The alteration for the worst which I discovered in your health the last time I had the pleasure of seeing you makes me sit down to take a survey with you of our approaching dissolution. The dream of life will soon be over; the morning of eternity will soon succeed. Away then with all the shadows of time! Away from them to the Eternal Substance—to Jesus, the first and the last—by Whom, and for Whom, all things consist.

We stand on the shore of a boundless ocean. Death, like a lion, comes to break our bones. Let us quietly strip ourselves of our mortal robes, that He may do with us as the Lord shall permit. In the mean while, let us step into the ark. Christ is the ark. My dear friend, believe in Jesus. Believe that your sins, red as crimson, are made white as snow by the superior tincture of His blood. Believe yourself into Christ. By simple faith, believe that He is your everlasting Head. Nor can you believe a lie, for God hath given that dear Savior to the worst of sinners to be received by a *lively* faith. He hath declared that it shall be done unto us according to our faith. If you simply take Jesus to be your Head, by the mystery of faith, you will be united to the resurrection and the life. The bitterness of death is past, my dear friend. Only look to Jesus. He died for you—died in your place—died under the frowns of Heaven, that we might die under its smiles. The Head was struck off that the members might be spared.

Stand, then, in Him. Be found in Him. Plead that He hath wrought a sinless righteousness for you, and hath more than sufficiently atoned for you by His cruel sufferings and ignominious death. Regard neither unbelief nor doubt. Fear neither sin nor hell. Choose neither life nor death. All these are swallowed up in the immensity of Christ and triumphed over in His cross. Believe that He hath made an end of sin, that you are comely in Him, that you are pardoned, accepted, and beloved of God in the one Mediator, Jesus Christ. Reason not with the law, but only with Him Who says, "Come and let us reason together; though your sins be as scarlet, they shall be as white as snow." Fight the good fight of faith. Hold fast your confidence in the atoning, sanctifying blood of the Lamb of God. Through His blood the accuser of the brethren is cast out. Confer no more with flesh and blood. Hunger and thirst after righteousness. Eat the flesh and drink the blood of the Redeemer; and live in Christ, that you may die in Him. Up and be doing the work of God. Believe in Him Whom He hath sent. Kiss the Son lest He be angry. Grasp Him as one who hath fallen into deep waters grasps the branch that hangs over him.

O slumber no more! Go meet the Bridegroom. Behold, He cometh! Trim your lamp. Hold up the vessel of your heart to the streaming wounds of Jesus, and it shall be filled with the oil of peace and gladness. Quit yourself like a soldier of Jesus. Look back to the world—the things and friends about you—no more. I entreat you, as a companion in tribulation; I charge you, as a minister, go, at every breath you draw, according to the grace and power given you, to the Physician Who gives nobody over—that says, "Him that cometh unto Me I will in no wise cast out;" and, "he that believeth in Him, though he were dead, yet shall he live."

E'er long there will be time no more. O my friend! Stir up yourself to lay hold on Him by faith and prayer. Let not those few sands that remain in your glass flow without the blood of Jesus. They are too precious to be offered up to slothful flesh, which is going to turn out its immortal inhabitant. Gladly resign your dust to the dust whence it was taken, and your spirit to Him Who gave and redeemed it. Look to Him, in spite of flesh and blood, of Satan and unbelief, and joyfully sing the believer's song, "O death, where is thy sting? O grave, where is thy victory? Thanks be to God, Who giveth us the victory, through our Lord Jesus Christ!" Let your surviving friends rejoice over you, as one faithful unto death—as one triumphing in death itself.

I am just informed of dear Miss Fragena's death. She caught a fever in visiting the poor, sick of that distemper, and lived a week to stand and rejoice in dying pains. As she lived, she died—a burning and a shining light. E'er long you will meet her in Abraham's bosom, whence she beckons you to follow her as she followed Christ. Be of good cheer, be not afraid. The same God Who helped her will carry you through. Your business is to commend yourself to Him—and to keep safe that which you commit to Him unto that day. To His faithfulness and love I commend you. I am, my dear friend, yours in Him.

To Mrs. Hatton

Madeley, Jan 30th, 1767

Dear Madam—I heard last night the news of Miss Hatton's death. As the stroke had long threatened you, and as she had, through mercy, long ago resigned herself to it, I hope it hath not found you without the shield of resignation, patience, and confidence in God. A sparrow, you know, falls not to the ground without His permission, much less can a member of His Son fall into the grave without His direction. Surely His wisdom is infallible. He hath chosen the better part both for you and your daughter. He hath chosen to take her out of her misery, to translate her to the place where the weary are at rest, and to give you, by removing her, an opportunity of caring for your soul as you cared for her body.

Now, what have you to do, Madam, but to put your hand upon your mouth and say, "It is the Lord. He gave, and He hath taken away; blessed be His holy Name!" If you sorrow, let it be in hope of meeting her soon, all glorious within and without, whom you lately saw such a spectacle of mortality. David observed in the lesson for this morning that the love of Jonathan had been better to him than the love of women. O dwell much upon the consideration of the love of Jesus, and you will find that it far surpasses that of the most dutiful children. Comfort yourself by the believing thought that Jesus lives, lives for you, and that your daughter lives in Him—where you will soon have the joy to meet her as an incarnate angel.

I am, with prayers for you and Miss Fanny, to whom I wish much consolation in her elder, never dying Brother, Dear Madam, your unworthy obliged servant in Christ.

To James Ireland

Madeley, Feb. 1767

My Very Dear Friend—The Lord will spare your daughter as long as she can get good, and do you and others good by the sight of her sufferings. When that cup is drunk up, she will be willing to go, and you to let her go. Remember she is the Lord's much more than yours; and that what we call dying is only breaking the shell of a troublesome body, that Christ may fully come at the kernel of the soul which He has bought.

Poor Miss Hatton died last Sunday fortnight full of serenity, faith, and love. The four last hours of her life were better than all her sickness. When the pangs of death were upon her, the comforts of the Almighty bore her triumphantly through, and some of her last words were: "Grieve not at my happiness; this world is no more to me than a bit of burnt paper. Grace! Grace! A sinner saved! I wish I could tell you half of what I feel and see. I am going to keep an everlasting Sabbath. O Death, where is thy sting? O grave, where is thy victory? Thanks be to God, Who giveth me the victory through my Lord Jesus Christ!"

It is very remarkable that she had hardly any joy in her illness; but God made her ample amends in her extremity. He kept the strongest cordial for the time of need. He does all things well. Blessed, for ever blessed, be His holy Name!

Worcestershire also lately lost a wise virgin of a truth, dear Miss Fragena, Mr. Biddulph's sister. The morning before she expired, she said, "I have had a stronger conflict last night than I ever had in all my life. It was sharp and terrible. But Jesus hath overcome, and He will also overcome for you and me. Be of good courage. Believe, hope, love, and obey."

I wish you had often such meetings as that you mention. Every one should have as many thrusts at that crooked serpent, that holy Devil, *Bigotry*, as he can. If I can leave my parish, I believe it will be to accompany Lady Huntingdon to the Goshen of our land—Yorkshire—to learn the love of Christ at the feet of my brethren and fathers there. I am obliged to you for the present you mention… Farewell in the Lord Jesus.

To James Ireland

Madeley, March 30th, 1767

MY VERY DEAR FRIEND—Yesterday I received your kind letter, and your kind present about a month ago. It came safe, and is a large stock for the poor and me. The Lord return it you in living water; may it flow like a never failing stream through your soul and those of all who are near and dear to you; that is, not only those who belong to your own household, but also to the household of faith. What a pleasure to love all, and to be a well wisher to all! …

To return to your present. I return you my sincere thanks for it, as well as for all your former favors, and for your kind offers of new ones. I have one to ask now, which is, that you would stay your hand and allow me to consume and wear out the old presents, without overcharging me with new ones. I do not say, stay your heart. No, let the oil of prayer flow from the cruise of your soul for me and mine till our poor vessels are filled with the oil of humble love.

What you say about Miss Ireland's filling puts me in mind of that worse disease of my heart, the dropsy of *self*. God gives me good physic and good food, but instead of digesting both properly, *self* retains what it should not. I *fill*, instead of remaining empty for fresh food. I lose my appetite, I swell, and am good for nothing but another operation. May the Lord so tap us that all our swelling may go down and return no more! The good Samaritan, Who is also a good Physician, wants to tap you spiritually by the bodily tapping of your daughter. To be cut in the fruit of our body is, sometimes, more painful than to be cut in our own body. May both she and you reap the fruit of the successful operation whenever it takes place! I am, with cordial affection, my dear sir, your very much obliged though very unworthy servant.

To George Whitefield

Madeley, May 18, 1767

Rev. and Dear Sir—I am confounded when I receive a letter from you. Present and eternal contempt from Christ and all His members is what I deserve. A sentence of death is my due; but, instead of it, I am favored with lines of love. God write a thousand, for them, upon your own heart! and help you to read, with still more triumphant and humbler demonstrations of gratitude, redeeming love, so deeply engraven upon the palms of our Savior's hands, and to assist many thousands more to spell out the mysterious words!

Your mentioning my poor ministrations among your congregation opens again a wound of shame that was but half healed. I feel the need of asking God, you, and your hearers pardon for weakening the glorious matter of the Gospel by my wretched, broken manner, and spoiling the heavenly power of it by the uncleanness of my heart and lips.

I should be glad to go and be your Curate some time this year. I see no opening, however, nor the least prospect of any. What between the dead and the living, a parish ties one down more than a wife. If I could go any where this year, it should be to Yorkshire to accompany Lady Huntingdon, according to a design that I had half formed last year; but I fear that I shall be debarred even from this. I set out tomorrow morning for Trevecka (God willing) to meet her Ladyship there and to show her the way to Madeley, where she proposes to stay three or four days in her way to Derbyshire. What Chaplain she will have there I know not; God will provide. I rejoice that though you are sure of Heaven, you have still a desire to inherit the earth by being a peace-maker. Somehow, you will enjoy the blessing that others may possibly refuse.

Last Sunday week Captain Scott preached to my congregation a sermon which was more blessed, though preached only upon my horse-block, than a hundred of those I preach in the pulpit. I invited him to come and treat her Ladyship next Sunday with another, now that the place is consecrated. If you should ever favor Shropshire with your presence, you shall have the Captain's or the Parson's pulpit at your option. Many ask me whether you will not come to have some fruit here also. What must I answer them? I, and many more, complain of a stagnation of the work. What must we do? Every thing buds and blossoms about us, yet our winter is not over.

I thought Mr. N———, who has been three weeks in Shropshire, would have brought the turtledove along with him; but I could not prevail upon him to come to this poor Capernaum. I think I hardly ever met his fellow for a judicious spirit. Still, what hath God done in him and me? I am out of hell, and mine eyes have seen also something of His salvation. Though I must and do gladly yield to him and all my brethren, yet I must and will contend that my being in the way to Heaven makes me as rich a monument of mercy as he or any of them. O that I may feel the wonderful effect of the patience that is manifested towards me! Lord, break me and make me a vessel capable of bearing Thy name, and the sweet savor of it, to my fellow-sinners!

Ask this for me, dear sir, and present my Christian respects to Mrs. Whitefield, Mr. Hardy and Keen, Mr. Joyce, Croom, and Wright. Tell Mr. Keen I am a letter in his debt and postponed writing it till I have had such a sight of Christ as to breathe His love through every line.

To James Ireland

Madeley, July 30th, 1768

Dear Sir—Uncertain as I am whether your daughter is yet alive, or whether the Lord hath called her from this vale of darkness and tears, I know not what to say to you on the subject, but this, that our heavenly Father appoints all things for the best. If her days of suffering are prolonged, it is to honor her with a conformity to the crucified Jesus. If they are shortened, she will have drunk all her cup of affliction. I flatter myself that she has found, at the bottom of it, not the bitterness and the gall of her sins, but the honey and wine of our divine Savior's righteousness, and the consolations of the Spirit.

I had lately some views of death, and it appeared to me in the most brilliant colors. What is it to die, but to open our eyes after the disagreeable dream of this life, after the black sleep in which we are buried on this earth? It is to break the prison of corruptible flesh and blood into which sin hath cast us. It is to draw aside the curtain, to cast off the material veil which prevents us from seeing the Supreme Beauty and Goodness face to face. It is to quit our polluted and tattered raiment, to be invested with robes of honor and glory. It is to behold the Sun of Righteousness in brightness without an interposing cloud. O my dear friend, how lovely is death when we look at it in Jesus Christ! To die is one of the greatest privileges of the Christian.

If Miss Ireland is still living, tell her a thousand times that Jesus is the Resurrection and the Life. He hath vanquished and disarmed death. He hath brought life and immortality to light. All things are ours, whether life or death, eternity or time. These are those great truths upon which she ought to risk, or rather to repose her soul with full assurance. Every thing is a shadow and a lie in comparison of the reality of the Gospel. If your daughter be dead, believe in Jesus, and you shall find her again in Him Who fills all in all, Who encircles the material and spiritual world in His arms—in the immense bosom of His Divinity.

I have not time to write to Mrs. Ireland; but I entreat her to keep her promise to inform me what victories she has gained over the world, the flesh, and sin. Surely when a daughter is dead or dying, it is high time for a father and a mother to die to all things below, and aspire, in good earnest, to that eternal life which God has given us in Jesus Christ. Adieu, my dear friend.

To Miss Ireland

Madeley, December 5, 1768

My Dear Afflicted Friend—I hear you are returned from the last journey you took in search of bodily health. Your heavenly Father sees fit to deny it you, not because He hateth you (for whom the Lord loveth He chasteneth), but because health and life might be fatal snares to your soul, out of which you could not escape but by tedious illness and an early death. Who knows also whether by all you have suffered, and still suffer, our gracious

Lord does not intend to kill you to the flesh and to the world, and both to you? Our hearts are so stupid, and our insensibility is so great, that the Father of our spirits sees it necessary to put some of His sharpest and longest thorns into our flesh, to make us go to our dear Jesus for the balmy graces of His Spirit.

I believe some are driven out of all the refuges of crafty and indolent nature only by the nearest and last approaches of that faithful minister and servant of Christ—Death. Of this I had a remarkable instance no longer ago than last Monday, when God took to Himself one of my poor afflicted parishioners, a boy of fifteen years of age, who was turned out of the infirmary two years ago as incurable. From that time he grew weaker every day by the running of a wound, but his poor soul did not gather strength. In many respects one would have thought his afflictions were lost upon him. He seemed to rest more in his sufferings and in his patience under them than in the Savior's blood and righteousness.

Being worn to a skeleton, he took to his deathbed. I found him there the week before last with his candle burning in the socket and no oil seemingly in the vessel. I spent an hour in setting before him the greatness of his guilt in this respect, that he had been so long under the rod of God and had not been whipped out of his careless unbelief to the bosom of Jesus Christ. He fell under the conviction, confessed that particular guilt, and began to call on the Lord with all the earnestness his dying frame would allow.

This was on the Wednesday. On the Wednesday following, the God Who delivers those that are appointed to die set one of his feet upon the Rock, and the next Sunday the other. He had chiefly used that short petition of the Lord's prayer, "Thy Kingdom come," and spent his last hours in testifying, as his strength would allow, that the Kingdom was come, and he was going to the King, to Whom he invited his joyful, mournful mother to make the best of her way after him.

Five or six days before his death, my wicked, unbelieving heart might have said, "To what purpose hath God afflicted so long and so heavily this poor worm?" But the Lord showed that He had been all that while driving in the spear of consideration and conviction, till at last it touched him in a sensible part and made him cry to the Savior in earnest. And who ever called upon Him in vain? No one. Not even that poor, indolent collier boy, who for two years would not so much as cross the way to hear me preach. Yet how good was the Lord! Because his body was too weak to bear any terrors in his mind, He showed him mercy without. The moment I heard him pray and saw him feel after a Savior, my fears on his account vanished. Though he had not been suffered to testify so clearly of God's Kingdom, yet I should have had a joyful hope that God had taken him Home.

Like the poor youth and myself, you have but one enemy, my dear friend—an indolent, unbelieving heart. The Lord hath driven it to a corner, however, to make you cry to Him Who has been waiting at the door all these years of trouble—waiting to bring you pardon, peace, and eternal life, in the midst of the pangs of bodily death. Jesus is His name. Salvation and love are His nature. He is the Father of eternity—your Father of course. All the love that is in Mr. Ireland's breast is nothing to the abyss of love that is in your Creator's heart. "A mother may forget her sucking child; but I will not forget thee," says He, to every poor, distressed soul that claims His help.

O fear not, my friend, to say, "I will arise and go to this Father, though I have sinned against Heaven and in His sight." Lo, He rises and runs to meet and embrace you. He hath already met you in the virgin's womb. There He did so cleave to your flesh and spirit that He assumed both, and wears them as a pledge of love to you. Claim, in return, claim, as you can, His blood and Spirit. Both are now the property of every dying sinner that is not above receiving by faith the unspeakable gift.

Your father has crossed the sea for you; Jesus has done more. He hath crossed the abyss that lies between Heaven and earth, between the Creator and the creature. He has waded through the sea of His tears, blood, and agonies, not to take you to the physician at Montpelier, but to become your Physician and

Savior Himself, to support you under all your bodily tortures, to sanctify all your extremities, and to heal your soul by His multiplied stripes. Your father has spared no expense to restore you to health; but Jesus, Who wants you in your prime, hath spared no blood in His veins to wash you from your sins, write your pardon, and seal your title to glory.

O my friend, delay not to cheerfully surrender yourself to this Good Shepherd. He will gladly lay you on the arm of His power, torn as you are with the bruises of sin and disease, and will carry you triumphantly to His heavenly sheepfold. Look not at your sins without beholding His blood and righteousness. Eye not death but to behold through that black door your gracious Savior, Who says, "Fear not, O thou of little faith; wherefore dost thou doubt?" Consider not eternity but as the palace where you are going to enter with the Bridegroom of souls and rest from all your sins and miseries.

View not the condemning law of God but as made honorable by Him Who was a curse for you and bore the malediction of the law by hanging, bleeding, and dying on the cursed tree in your place. If you think of hell, let it be to put you in mind to believe that the blood of God incarnate hath quenched its devouring flames. If you have no comfort, mistrust not Jesus on that account. On the contrary, take advantage from it to give greater glory to God by believing, as Abraham, in hope against hope. And let this be your greatest comfort, that Jesus, Who had all faith and patience, cried for you in His dying moments, "My God, My God, why hast Thou forsaken me?"

As your strength will bear exertion, and His grace apprehended will allow, surrender yourself constantly to Him as the purchase of His blood. Invite Him earnestly to you as a poor worm perishing without Him. In this simple, Gospel way, wait the Lord's leisure, and He will comfort your heart. He will make all His goodness to pass before you here, or take you hence to show you what you could not bear in flesh and blood—the direct beams of the uncreated beauty of your heavenly Spouse.

I hope you take care to have little or nothing else mentioned to and about you but His praises and promises. Your tongue and ears are going to be silent in the grave; now, or never, use them to hear and speak good of His name. Comfort your weeping friends. Reprove the backsliders. Encourage seekers. Water, and you shall be watered. Death upon you makes you, through Christ, a mother in Israel. Arise, as Deborah. Remember the praying, believing, preaching, though dying thief; and be not afraid to drop a word for Him Who openeth a fountain of blood for you in His dying, tortured body. Suffer, live, die, at His feet, and you will soon revive, sing, and reign in His bosom for evermore. Farewell in the Conqueror of death and Prince of Life.

To James Ireland

Madeley, March 26th, 1769

My Dear Friend—The Lord is desirous of making you a true disciple of His dear Son, the Man of Sorrows, by sending you affliction upon affliction. A sister and a wife who appear to hasten to the grave, in which you have so lately laid your only daughter, place you in circumstances of uncommon affliction. But in this see the finger of Him Who works all in all, and Who commands us to forsake all to follow Him. Believe in Him. Believe that He does all for the best—that all shall work for good to those who love Him—and you shall see the salvation of God; and with your temptations and trials, He shall open a door of deliverance for you and yours. His goodness to your daughter ought to encourage your faith and confidence for Mrs. Ireland. Offer her upon the altar, and you shall see that if it be best for her and you, His grace will suspend the blow which threatens you.

Your rich present of meal came last week and shall be distributed to the pious poor agreeably to your orders, as a proof that Jesus, the liberal Jesus, the Bread of Life, is risen indeed and lives in His members, who mutually aid and comfort each other. We are happy to receive your bounty, but you are more happy in bestowing it upon us; witness the words of Jesus: "It is more blessed to give than to receive." Nevertheless, receive by faith the presents of the Lord, the gifts of His Spirit, and reject not the Bread which cometh down from Heaven, because the Lord gives it you with so much love. Adieu. The God of peace be with you, and prepare you for whatever it shall please Him to appoint!

To James Ireland

Madeley, May 17th, 1769

My Dear Friend—I sympathize with you with all my heart, and I pray that you may have patience and wisdom proportioned to your difficulties. You must take up your cross and pray in secret, like a man whose earthly cisterns are broken on every side, and who hath need of consolation from feeling the fountain of living waters springing up in his soul unto eternal life. I have every moment need to follow the advice I give to you, but my carnal mind makes strong resistance. I must enter into life by death. I must be crucified on the cross of Christ before I can live by the power of His resurrection. The Lord give us grace to die to ourselves, for it is not enough to die to our relatives. Blessed indeed is that union with Jesus Christ by which a believer can cast upon that Rock of Ages not only his burdens, but himself—the heaviest burden of all. O Lord, give us power to believe with that faith which works by the prayer of confidence and love!

To a Friend

My Dear Friend—My delay has, I hope, driven you to the Lord, Who is our Urim and Thummim, Whose answers are infallibly true and just. Not so those of men. Nevertheless, the Lord generally helps us by each other. May He, therefore, help you by these lines.

You got safe out of Egypt with gladness, and now you seem entangled in the wilderness. But it may be needful for the trial of your faith, patience, self-denial, etc., that you should be left for a while to feel your own barrenness. Therefore hold fast what you have till the Lord comes with more, equally avoiding *discouraging thoughts* and *slight indifference*. Retire more inwardly, and quietly listen to what the Lord will say concerning you, refusing creature comforts and acting faith in God your Creator, Christ your Redeemer, and the Spirit your Comforter.

You have always a feeling which, properly attended to, would make you shout, "I am, I am out of hell!" I beg that this wonderful mercy may not appear cheap to you. If it does, you have got up, and must come down; for it is proper that the Lord should bring down your spirit and keep you upon crumbs till you have learned to be thankful for them.

At the first reading of your letter these things struck me: (1) You are wanting in the venture of faith. You do not give enough to that kind of implicit confidence in Christ which says, "I will trust in Thee though Thou slay me." Now this is a lesson which you must learn. Sink or swim, a believer must learn to cast himself headlong into the boundless sea of divine truth and love. (2) You have not learned to hold fast what you have, and to be thankful for it, till the Lord comes with more—till he baptizes you with the Holy Ghost and with fire. (3) You do not make a proper use of the *joy of hope*, which, nevertheless, is to be your strength till the Lord comes to His temple to make His abode there. Adieu.

TO MR. HENRY BROOKE

Madeley, Sept. 6th, 1772

DEAR SIR—I thankfully accept the pleasure, profit, and honor of your correspondence. But I must not deceive you: I have not yet learned the blessed precept of our Lord in respect of writing and receiving letters. I still find it more blessed to receive than to give. And till I have got out of that selfishness, never depend on a letter from me till you see it. But be persuaded, nevertheless, that one from you will always be welcome.

I see by your works that you love truth, and that you will force your way through all the barriers of prejudice to embrace it in its meanest dress. That makes me love. I hope to improve by your example and your lessons. One thing I want truly to learn, that is, that creatures and visible things are but *shadows*, and that God is God, Jehovah, the true eternal substance. To live practically in this truth is to live in the suburbs of Heaven. Really to believe that in God we live, move, and have our being is to find and enjoy the root of our existence. It is to slide from self into our original principle, from the carnal into the spiritual, from the visible into the invisible, from time into eternity.

Give me, at your leisure, some directions how to cease from busying myself about the husk of things, and how I shall break through the shell till I come to the kernel of resurrection life and power that lies hid from the unbeliever's sight. You mention "A short sketch of your path already passed, and of your present feelings." I believe it will be profitable to me for instruction and reproof; therefore, I shall gladly accept it.

Pray, my dear Sir, about feelings… I have often thought that some of the feelings you describe depend a good deal upon the fineness of the nerves and bodily organs. And as I am rather of a Stoic turn, I have sometimes comforted myself in thinking that my want of feelings might, in a degree, proceed from the dullness of Swiss nerves. If I am not mistaken, Providence directs me to you to have this important question solved. May not some persons have as much true faith, love, humanity, and pity as others who are ten times more affected, at least for a season? And what directions would you give to a Christian Stoic, if these two ideas are not absolutely incompatible. My stoicism helps me, I think, to weather out a storm of displeasure which my little pamphlets have raised against me. You see, I at once consult you as an old friend and spiritual casuist, nor know I how to testify better to you how unreservedly I begin to be, my very dear friend, Yours in the Lord.

TO MR. WESLEY

Madeley, Feb. 6, 1773

REV. AND DEAR SIR—I hope the Lord, Who has so wonderfully stood by you hitherto, will preserve you to see many of your sheep, and me among them, enter into rest. Should Providence call you first, I shall do my best, by the Lord's assistance, to help your brother to gather the wreck and keep together those who are not absolutely bent to throw away the Methodist doctrines and discipline, as soon as he that now letteth is removed out of the way. Every help will then be necessary, and I shall not be backward to throw in my mite.

In the meantime, you sometimes need an assistant to serve tables and occasionally fill up a gap. Providence visibly appointed me to that office many years ago. And though it no less evidently called me hither, yet I have not been without doubts, especially for some years past, whether it would not be expedient that I should resume my office as your deacon. Not that I have any view of presiding over the Methodists after you, but to ease you a little in your old age and to be in the way of receiving, perhaps doing, more good.

I have sometimes thought how shameful it was that no clergyman should join you to keep in the church the work God has enabled you to carry on therein. And as the little estate I have in my own country is sufficient for my maintenance, I have thought I would one day or other offer you and the Methodists my free service. While my love of retirement made me linger, I was providentially led to do something on Lady Huntingdon's plan. But being shut out there, it appears to me I am again called to my first work. Nevertheless, I would not leave this place without a fuller persuasion that the time is quite come. Not that God uses me much here, but I have not yet sufficiently cleared my conscience from the blood of all men.

Meantime I beg the Lord to guide me by His counsel and make me willing to go any where or no where, to be any thing or nothing. Help by your prayers, till you can bless by word of mouth, Rev. and dear Sir, your willing though unprofitable servant in the Gospel.

To Mr. Vaughan

Madeley, Feb. 11th, 1773

My Very Dear Friend—Your kind letter I received in the beginning of the week, and your kind present at the end of it. For both I heartily thank you. Nevertheless, I could wish it were your last present, for I find it more blessed to give than to receive; and in point of the good things of this life, my body does not want much, and I can do with what is more common, and cheaper than the rarities you ply me with.

Your bounty reminds me of the repeated mercies of our God. They follow one another as wave does wave at sea—and all to waft us to the pleasing shore of confidence and gratitude, where we cannot only cast anchor near, but calmly stand on the Rock of Ages, and defy the rage of tempests. But you complain that you are not *there*: billows of temptation drive you from the haven where you would be, and you cry out still, "O wretched man! who shall deliver me?"

Here I would ask, Are you willing, *really willing* to be delivered? Is your sin, is the prevalence of temptation, a burden too heavy for you to bear? If it is, if your complaint is not a kind of religious compliment, be of good cheer, only believe. Look up, for your redemption draws near. He is near that delivers, that justifies, that sanctifies you. Cast your soul upon Him. An act of faith will help you to a lift, but *one act* of faith will not do. *Faith must be our life*, I mean, *in conjunction with its Grand Object*. You cannot live by one breath; you must breathe on, and draw the electric, vital fire into your lungs together with the air. So you must believe and draw the divine power, and the fire of Jesu's love, together with the truth of the Gospel, which is the blessed element in which believers live…

Beware of the world. If you have losses, be not cast down, nor root in the earth with more might and main to repair them. If prosperity smiles upon you, you are in double danger. Think, my friend, that earthly prosperity is like a colored cloud, which passes away and is soon lost in the shades of night and death. Beware of hurry. Martha, Martha, one thing is needful. Choose it, stand to your choice, and the good part shall not be taken from you by sickness or death. God bless you and yours with all that makes for His glory and your peace! I am, my dear friend, yours, etc.

To James Ireland

Madeley, September 1, 1773

My Very Dear Friend—I see life so short, and that time passes away with such rapidity, that I should be very glad to spend it in solemn prayer; but it is necessary that a man should have some exterior occupation. The chief thing is to employ ourselves profitably. My throat is not formed for the labors of preaching. When I have preached three or four times together, it inflames and fills up; and the efforts which I am then obliged to make in speaking heat my blood. Thus I am, by nature, as well as by the circumstances I am in, obliged to employ my time in writing a little. O that I may be enabled to do it to the glory of God! Let us love this good God, Who hath "so loved the world that He gave His only begotten Son, that we might not perish, but have everlasting life." How sweet is it, when on our knees, to receive this Jesus, this heavenly Gift, and to offer our praises and thanks to our heavenly Father! The Lord teaches me four lessons: The first is to be thankful that I am not in hell. The second, to become nothing before Him. The third, to receive the Gift of God—the person of Jesus. The fourth, to feel my need of the Spirit of Jesus, and to wait for it. These four lessons are very deep. O when shall I have learned them! Let us go together to the school of Jesus and learn to be meek and lowly in heart. Adieu.

To James Ireland

Madeley, March 27th, 1774

My Dear Sir— … I have just spirit enough to enjoy my solitude, and to bless God that I am out of the hurry of the world—even of the spiritual world. I tarry gladly in my Jerusalem till the Kingdom of God comes with power. Till then it matters not where I am; only as my chief call is here, here I gladly stay, till God fits me for the pulpit or the grave. I still spend my mornings in scribbling. Though I grudge so much time in writing, yet a man must do something, and I may as well investigate truth as do anything else, except solemn praying and visiting my flock. I shall be glad to have done with my present avocation, so that I may give myself up more to those two things.

O how life goes! I walked, now I gallop into eternity. The bowl of life goes rapidly down the steep hill of time. Let us be wise. Embrace we Jesus and the resurrection. Let us trim our lamps and give ourselves afresh to Him that bought us, till we can do it without reserve. Adieu.

To Charles Wesley

Madeley, Jan. 1775

My Very Dear Sir—I am glad you did not altogether disapprove my *Essay on Truth*. The letter, I grant, profiteth little until the Spirit animates it. I had, some weeks ago, one of those touches which realize, or rather spiritualize, the letter; and it convinced me more than ever that what I say in that tract of the Spirit and of Faith is truth. I am also persuaded that the Faith and Spirit which belong to perfect Christianity are at a very low ebb, even among believers. When the Son of Man cometh to set up His Kingdom, shall He find Christian faith upon the earth? Yes, but I fear as little as He found of Jewish faith when He came in the flesh.

I believe you cannot rest either with the easy Antinomian or the busy Pharisee. You and I have nothing to do but to die to all that is of sinful nature and to pray for the power of an endless life. God make us faithful to our convictions and keep us from the snares of outward things. You are in danger from music, children, poetry; and I from speculation, controversy, sloth, etc., etc. Let us watch against the deceitfulness of self and sin in all their appearances.

What power of the Spirit do you find among the believers in London? What openings of the Kingdom? Is the well springing up in many hearts? Are many souls dissatisfied, and looking for the Kingdom of God in power? Watchman, what of the night? What of the day? What of the dawn?

I feel the force of what you say in your last about the danger of so encouraging the inferior dispensation as to make people rest short of the faith which belongs to perfect Christianity. I have tried to obviate it in some parts of the *Equal Check*, and hope to do it more effectually in my reply to Mr. Hill's *Creed for Perfectionists*. I expect a letter from you on the subject. Write with openness, and do not fear to discourage me by speaking your disapprobation of what you dislike. My aim is to be found at the feet of all, bearing and forbearing until truth and love bring better days. I am, Rev. and dear Sir, your most affectionate brother and son in the Gospel.

To Charles Wesley

Madeley, Dec. 4th, 1775

My Very Dear Brother—I see the end of my controversial race, and I have such courage to run it out, that I think it my bounden duty to run and strike my blow and fire my gun before the water of discouragement has quite wetted the gunpowder of my activity. This makes me seem to neglect my dearest correspondents.

Old age comes faster upon me than upon you. I am already so gray-headed that I wrote to my brother to know if I am not fifty-six instead of forty-six. The wheel of time moves so rapidly that I seem to be in a new element; and yet, praised be God, my strength is preserved far better than I could expect. I came home last night at eleven o'clock tolerably well after reading prayers, preaching twice, and giving the sacrament in my own church. Then I had preached again and met a few people in society at the next market town.

The Lord is wonderfully gracious to me; and, what is more to me than many favors, He helps me to see His mercies in a clearer light. In years past, I did not dare to be thankful for mercies which now make me shout for joy. I had been taught to call them *common mercies*, and I made as little of them as apostates do of the blood of Christ when they call it a *common thing*. But now the veil begins to rend. I invite you and all the world to praise God for His patience, truth, and loving kindness, which have followed me all my days, and prevented me, not only in the night watches, but in the past ages of eternity. O how I hate the delusion which has robbed me of so many comforts! Farewell. I am, etc.

To Mrs. Mary Cartwright

Madeley, 1775

My Dear Friend—As it may be long before you have an opportunity to hear a sermon, I find myself drawn by friendship and pastoral care to send you a few lines to meditate upon tomorrow.

As I was longing for an opportunity to offer life, friends, and liberty to Him Who is worth a thousand such *alls*, I thought I must wait for no other opportunity, and found another blessing in using the present moment. I did not forget to offer you among my friends, and I found it on my mind to pray and praise with you, and to beseech you to fulfill my joy by giving me to see you all glorious within and full of eager desire to be with our everlasting Friend. O let us take a thousand times more notice of Him, till the thought of Him engrosses all other thoughts, the desire of Him all other desires.

Nothing can reconcile me to let my friends go but the fullest evidence that they are going to Jesus. If you go before me, let me not want that comfort. Let me never see you, but full of an earnest desire to do and suffer the will of our God. I wanted to see heavenly joy and glory beaming from your eyes last night, and I feared I saw them not. Pardon my fears if they have no foundation. Charity thinks no evil, hopes all, and yet is jealous with a godly jealousy. And the warmer the charity, the stronger and keener the jealousy. A doubt passed through my mind whether you had not caught our dullness, whether your soul is as near to God as it was some weeks ago. O! if the multiplied mercies of God toward us do not rouse us to the third heaven of gratitude, what will?

My prayer, my ardent prayer to God, and I make it now afresh with tears of desire, is that you may live as one who does not depend on another breath. Come, my dear friend, up with your heart and spread the arms of your faith. Welcome Jesus. Believe till you are drawn above yourself and earth—till your flaming soul mounts, and loses itself in the Sun of Righteousness. I want you to be a burning, shining light, setting fire to all the thatch of the Devil and kindling every smoking flax around you. Disappoint not the Savior's hope, and mine. I expect to see you not only a risen Lazarus, and a spared Hezekiah, but a Mary at Jesus' feet, a Deborah in the work of the Lord. There is what St. Paul calls a being *beside ourselves*, which becomes you so much the better as you are restored to us against hope—and for how long we know not.

Fulfill my joy, I say, which must droop till I can rejoice over you living, dying, or dead, with joy unspeakable and full of glory. Give yourself much to believing, thankful, solemn prayer. I was condemned for not making more of the solemn opportunity I had with you last Thursday. O! if we are spared to meet again, let us pray until we wind our hearts into ardent praise; and then, let us praise till we are caught up into Heaven. Hold up our hands tomorrow; and if we meet on Monday, be it in the name of Christ to pour the oil of joy into each other's hearts by confessing

Him more heartily our God, our life, our present and never dying Friend. Farewell in Him every way.

To James Ireland

Madeley, Feb. 3rd, 1776

My Very Dear Friend—Upon the news of your illness, I and many more helped to pray that you might be supported under your pressures, and that they might yield the peaceable fruit of righteousness. We shall now turn our prayers into praises for your happy recovery, and for the support the Lord has granted you under your trial. May it now appear that you imitate David, who said, "It was good for me that I was afflicted." Let people say what they will, there are lessons which we can never learn but under the cross. We must suffer with Christ if we will be glorified with Him. I hope you will take care that it may not be said of you as it was of Hezekiah, "He rendered not unto the Lord according to the benefit" of his recovery. Let us rather say, "What shall I render unto the Lord for all His benefits?" And may we see the propriety and profit of rendering Him our bodies and souls—the sacrifices of humble, praising, obedient love, and warm, active, cheerful thanksgiving.

My little political piece is published in London. You thank me for it beforehand; I believe they are the only thanks I shall have. It is well you sent them before you read the book; and yet, whatever contempt it brings upon me, I still think I have written the truth. If you did read my publications, I would beg you to cast a look upon that, and reprove what appears to you amiss; for if I have been wrong in writing, I hope I shall not be so excessively wrong as not to be thankful for any reproof candidly leveled at what I have written. I prepare myself to be like my Lord, in my little measure—I mean, to be despised and rejected of men, a man of sorrows and acquainted with griefs—most reviled for what I mean best. The Lord strengthen you in body and soul, to do and suffer His will. Adieu.

TO JOSEPH BENSON

Madeley, February, 1776

MY VERY DEAR BROTHER—I have long wished to hear from you. If I remember right, when you wrote me a few lines from Leeds, you intimated that you would let me hear from you more fully. Either my hopes have dreamed it, or your many avocations have as yet prevented your indulging me with a line. Be that as it will, I send this to inquire after your welfare in every sense, and to let you know that though I am pretty well in body, I break fast—that I want to break faster in spirit than I do. Blessed be God, I have been put into such pinching, grinding circumstances for near a year, by a series of providential and domestic trials, as have given me some deadly blows. May the wounds be never healed! May all the life of self, which is the vital blood of the old Adam, flow out at the cuts.

I am not without hopes of setting my eyes on you once more. Mr. Wesley kindly invited me some weeks ago to travel with him and visit some of the Societies. The controversy is partly over, and I feel an inclination to break one of my chains (parochial retirement) which may be a nest for self. A young minister in deacon's orders has offered to be my curate; and if he can live in this wilderness, I shall have some liberty to leave it. I commit the matter entirely to the Lord. To lie at the beck of Providence, to do or not to do, to have or not to have, is, I think (in such cases), a becoming frame of mind…

The few professors I see in these parts are so far from what I could wish them and myself to be that I cannot but cry out, "Lord, how long wilt Thou give Thine heritage to desolation or barrenness? How long shall the heathen say, 'Where is now their indwelling God?'" I hope it is better with you in the North. I have got acquainted by letter with a sensible man who calls himself "an expectant of the Kingdom of God," with whom (so far as I know) I perfectly agree. He is a Nathaniel and a Simeon indeed. You would love him if you knew him.

I look upon your discoveries in the field and mines of truth as mine. I hope you will not deprive me of what I have a right to share in, according to the old rule, "they had all things common." What are your heart, your pen, your tongue doing? Are they receiving, sealing, spreading the truth every where within your sphere? Are you dead to praise or dispraise? Could you quietly pass for a mere fool and have gross nonsense fathered upon you without any uneasy reflection of self? The Lord bless you. The Lord make you a child and a father. Beware of your grand enemy—earthly wisdom and unbelieving reasonings. You will never overcome but by childlike, loving simplicity. Adieu.

To Joseph Benson

Madeley, March, 1776

My Very Dear Brother— ... I see so little fruit in these parts that I am almost disheartened, both with respect to the power of the Word and the experience of the professors I converse with. I am closely followed with the thought that the Kingdom in the Holy Ghost is almost lost and that faith in the dispensation of the Spirit is at a very low ebb. But it may be, I think so, on account of my little experience and the weakness of the faith of those I converse with. It may be better in all other places. I shall be glad to travel a little to see the goodness of the land. God deliver us from all extremes and make and keep us humble, loving, disinterested, and zealous!

I have almost run my race of scribbling. I preached before Mr. Greaves came as much as my strength could well admit, although to little purpose. But I must not complain. If one person receive a good desire in ten years, by my instrumentality, it is a greater honor than I deserve—an honor for which I should think I could not be too thankful, if my mind were as low as it ought to be. Let us bless the Lord for all things. We have reasons innumerable to do it. Bless Him on my account as well as your own, and the God of peace be with you. Do not forget to ask that He may be with your sincere friend.

TO MR. VAUGHAN

Madeley, March 21st, 1776

DEAR SIR— … I thought I should soon have done with controversy, but now I give up the hope of having done with it before I die. There are three sorts of people I must continually attack or defend myself against: Gallios, Pharisees, and Antinomians. I hope I shall die in this harness, fighting against some of them. I do not, however, forget that the Gallio, the Simon, and the Nicolas within are far more dangerous to me than those without. In my own heart, that immense field, I must first fight the Lord's battles and my own. Help me here. Join me in this field. All Christians are here militiamen, if they are not professed soldiers. O, my friend, I need wisdom—meekness of wisdom! A heart full of it is better than all your cider-vault full of the most generous liquors; and it is in Christ for us. O go and ask for you and me, and I shall ask for myself and you. What a mercy it is that our Lord bears stock! May we not be ashamed nor afraid to come and beg every moment for wine and milk, grace and wisdom.

Beware, my friend, of the world. Let not its cares, nor the deceitfulness of its riches, keep or draw you from Jesus. Before you handle the birdlime, be sure you dip your heart and hand in the oil of grace. Time flies. Years of plenty and of scarcity, of peace and of war, disappear before the eternity to which we are all hastening. May we see now the winged dispatch of time as we shall see it in a dying hour. By coming to and abiding in Christ, our fortress and city of refuge, may we be enabled to bid defiance to our last enemy. Christ has fully overcome him; and by the victory of the Head, the living members cannot but be fully victorious.

To Charles Wesley

Madeley, May 11th, 1776

My Dear Brother—What are you doing in London? Are you ripening as fast for the grave as I am? How we should lay out every moment for God! Thank God, I look at our last enemy with great calmness. I hope, however, that the Lord will spare me to publish my end of the controversy, which is, *A Double Dissertation upon the Doctrines of Grace and Justice*. This piece will, I flatter myself, reconcile all the candid Calvinists and candid Arminians, and be a means of pointing out the way in which peace and harmony might be restored to the Church.

I still look for an outpouring of the Spirit, inwardly and outwardly. Should I die before that great day, I shall have the consolation to see it from afar, like Abraham and the Baptist, and to point it out to those who shall live when God does this.

Thank God, I enjoy uninterrupted peace in the midst of my trials, which are sometimes not a few. Joy also I possess, but I look for a joy of a superior nature. The Lord bestow it when and how He pleaseth! I thank God, I feel myself in a good degree dead to praise and dispraise; I hope, at least, that it is so, because I do not feel that the one lifts me up, or that the other dejects me. I want to see a Pentecostal Christian Church. If it be not to be seen at this time upon earth, I am willing to go and see this glorious wonder in Heaven. How is it with you? Are you ready to seize the crown in the name of the Redeemer reigning in your heart? We run a race towards the grave. John is likely to outrun you unless you have a swift foot. The Lord grant we may sink deeper into the Redeemer's grave, and there live and die, and gently glide into our own…

Let us pray that God would renew our youth as that of the eagle so that we may bear fruit in our old age. The Lord strengthen you to the last! I hope I shall see you again before my death. If not, let us rejoice at the thought of meeting in Heaven. Give my kind love to Mrs. Wesley, to my god-daughter and her brothers, who all, I hope, remember their Creator in the days of their youth. Adieu.

To Charles Wesley

Madeley, Sept. 15th, 1776

My Very Dear Brother—I lately consulted a pious gentleman near Lichfield who is famous for his skill in the disorders of the breast. He assured me that I am in no immediate danger of a consumption of the lungs, and that my disorder is upon the nerves in consequence of too much close thinking. He permitted me to write and preach in moderation, and gave me medicines which, I think, are of service in taking off my feverish heats. My spitting of blood is stopped, and I may yet be spared to travel with you as an invalid.

If God add one inch to my span, I see my calling. I desire to know nothing but Christ, and Him crucified, revealed in the Spirit. I long to feel the utmost power of the Spirit's dispensation, and I will endeavor to bear my testimony to the glory of that dispensation both with my pen and tongue. Some of our injudicious or inattentive friends will probably charge me with novelty for it. Be that as it will, let us meekly stand for the truth as it is in Jesus and trust the Lord for every thing.

I thank God that I feel myself so dead to popular applause that, I trust, I should not be afraid to maintain a truth against all the world; and yet I dread to dissent from any child of God, and am ready to condescend to every one. O what depths of humble love, what heights of Gospel truth do I sometimes see! I want to sink into the former and rise into the latter. Help me by your example, letters, and prayers. Let us, after our forty years' abode in the wilderness with Moses and John, break forth after our Joshua into the Canaan of pure love.

To the Parishioners of Madeley

Newington, Dec. 28th, 1776

My Dear Parishioners—I hoped to have spent the Christmas holidays with you and to have ministered to you in holy things. The weakness of my body confining me here, however, I humbly submit to the divine dispensation, and ease the trouble of my absence by being present with you in spirit and by reflecting on the pleasure I have felt, in years past, while singing with you, "Unto us a child is born, unto us a son is given," etc. This truth is as important now as it was then, and as worthy to be thankfully received at Newington as at Madeley. Let us, then, receive it with all readiness and it will unite us. We shall meet in Christ, the center of lasting union, the source of true life, and the spring of pure righteousness and joy. Then our hearts shall be full of the song of angels, "Glory be to God on high! Peace on earth! Goodwill towards each other, and all mankind."

In order to this, may the eye of your understanding be more and more opened to see your need of a Redeemer and to behold the suitableness, freeness, and fullness of the redemption which was wrought out by the Son of God, and which is applied by the Spirit through faith. The wish which glows in my soul is so ardent and powerful that it brings me down on my knees while I write; and, in that supplicating posture, I entreat you all to consider and improve the day of your visitation and to prepare in good earnest to meet with joy your God and your unworthy pastor in another world.

Weak as I was when I left Madeley, I hear that several who were then young, healthy, and strong, have got the start of me—that some have been hurried into eternity without being indulged with a moment's warning. May the awful accident strike a deeper consideration into all our souls. May the sound of their bodies, dashed to pieces at the bottom of a pit, rouse us to a speedy conversion, that we may never fall into the bottomless pit, and that iniquity and delays may not be our eternal ruin. Tottering as I stand on the brink of the grave, some of you who seem far from it may drop into it before me; for what has happened may happen still.

Let us, then, all awake out of sleep. Let us all prepare for our approaching change and give ourselves no rest till we have got Gospel ground to hope that our great change will be a happy one. In order to this, I beseech you, by all the ministerial and providential calls you have had for these seventeen years, harden not your hearts. Let the longsuffering of God towards us who survive the hundreds I have buried lead us all to repentance. Dismiss your sins. Embrace Jesus Christ, Who wept for you in the manger, bled for you in Gethsemane, hung for you on the cross, and now pleads for you on His mediatorial Throne.

By all that is near and dear to you, as men and as Christians, meet me not, on the great day, in your sins and in your blood, enemies to Christ by unbelief, and to God by wicked works. Meet me in the garment of repentance, in the robe of Christ's merits, and in the white linen (the purity of heart and life) which is the holiness of the godly—that holiness without which no man shall see God. Let the time past suffice in which some of you have lived in sin. By repentance put off the old man and his works; by faith put on the Lord Jesus and His righteousness. Let all the wickedness be gone—for ever gone—with the old year. With the New Year begin a new life—a life of renewed devotion to God and increasing love to our neighbor.

The sum of all I have preached to you is contained in the following four propositions: First, heartily repent of your sins, original and actual. Secondly, believe the Gospel of Christ in sincerity and truth. Thirdly, in the power which true faith gives (for all things commanded are possible to him that believeth), run with humble confidence the way of God's commandments before God and men. Fourthly, by continuing to take up your cross and by continuing to receive the pure milk of God's Word, grow in grace and in the knowledge of Jesus Christ. So shall you grow in peace and joy all the days of your life; and when rolling years shall be lost in eternity, you will for ever grow in bliss and heavenly glory.

O what bliss! What glory! The Lord shall be our Sun and our crown; and we shall be jewels in each other's crown, I in yours and you in mine. For ever we shall be with the Lord and with one another. We shall all live in God's heavenly Church, the Heaven of heavens. All our days will be a Sabbath, and our Sabbath eternity. No bar of business or sickness, no distance of time nor place, no gulf of death or the grave shall part us more. We shall meet in the bosom of Abraham, who met Christ in the bosom of divine love. O what a meeting! And shall some of us meet there this very year which we are just entering upon? What a year! On that blessed year, if we are of the number of those who die in the Lord, our souls shall burst the womb of this corruptible flesh. We shall be born into the other world. We shall behold the Sun of Righteousness without a cloud and for ever bask in the beams of His glory. Is not this prospect glorious enough to make us bid defiance to sin and the grave—to make us join the cry of the Spirit and the Bride, "Come, Lord Jesus, come quickly," though it should be in the black chariot of death?

Should God bid me to stay on earth a little longer to serve you in the Gospel of His Son; should He renew my strength (for no word is impossible with Him) to do among you the work of a pastor, I hope I shall, by God's grace, prove a more humble, zealous, and diligent minister than I have hitherto been. Some of you have supposed that I made more ado about eternity and your precious souls than they were worth, but how great was your mistake! Alas! It is my grief and shame that I have not been, both in public and private, a thousand times more earnest and importunate with you about your spiritual concerns.

Pardon me, my dear friends, pardon me my ignorances and negligences in this respect. And as I most humbly ask your forgiveness, so I most heartily forgive any of you who may at any time have made no account of my little labors. I only entreat such now to evidence a better mind by paying a double attention to the loud warnings of Providence, and to the pathetic discourses of the faithful minister who now supplies my place. And may God, for Christ's sake, forgive us all, as we forgive one another!

The more nearly I consider death and the grave, judgment and eternity, the more, blessed be God, I feel that I have preached to you the truth, and that the truth is solid as the Rock of ages. Glory be to His divine grace that I can say, in some degree, "Here is firm footing." Follow me; and the sorrows of death, instead of encompassing you around, will keep at an awful distance, and, with David, we shall follow our great Shepherd even through the dreary valley without fearing or feeling any evil.

Although I hope to see much more of the goodness of the Lord in the land of the living than I do see; yet, blessed be the divine mercy, I see enough to keep my mind at all times unruffled and to make me willing to calmly resign my soul into the hands of my faithful Creator, my loving Redeemer, and my sanctifying Comforter, this moment or the next, if He call for it. I desire your public thanks for all the favors He showeth me continually with respect to both my soul and body. Help me to be thankful, for it is a pleasant thing to be thankful. May our thankfulness crown the New Year as God's patience and goodness have crowned all our life. Permit me to bespeak an interest in your prayers also. Ask that my faith may be willing to receive all that God's grace is willing to bestow. Ask that I may meekly suffer and zealously do all the will of God in my present circumstances, and that, living or dying, I may say with the witness of God's Spirit, "For me to live is Christ, and to die is gain."

If God call me soon from earth, I beg He may, in His good providence, appoint a more faithful shepherd over you. You need not fear that He will not. You see that for these many months you have not only had no famine of the Word, but the richest plenty; and what God has done for months, He can do for years—yea, for all the years of your life. Only pray. "Ask and you shall receive." Meet at the Throne of Grace and you shall meet at the Throne of Glory your affectionate, obliged, and unworthy minister.

To the Parishioners of Madeley

Newington, Jan. 13th, 1777

My Dear Companions in Tribulation—All the children of God I love. My delight is in them that excel in strength, and my tenderest compassions move towards those that exceed in weakness. But of all the children of God, none have so great a right to my peculiar love as you. Your stated or occasional attendance on my poor ministry, the countless thousands of steps you have taken to hear the Word of our common Lord from my despised pulpit, the bonds of neighborhood, and the many happy hours I have spent before the Throne of Grace with you all, endear you peculiarly to me.

With tears of grateful joy I recollect the awful moments when we have, in the strength of our dear Redeemer, bound ourselves to stand to our baptismal vow—to renounce all sin, to believe all the articles of the Christian faith, and to keep God's commandments to the end of our life—especially the new commandment, which enjoins us to love one another as Christ has loved us.

O! my dear brethren, let this repeated vow, so reasonable, so just, and so comfortable, appear to us worthy of our greatest regard. For my own part, asking pardon of God and you all for not having exulted more in the privilege of keeping that vow every day better and of loving you every hour more tenderly, I am not at all discouraged. But I determine with new courage and delight to love my neighbor as myself, and to love our Covenant God—Father, Son, and Holy Ghost—with all my mind, heart, and strength—with all the powers of my understanding, will, and affections. This resolution is bold, but it is *evangelical*, being equally founded on the precept and promise of our Lord Jesus Christ, Whose cleansing blood can atone for all our past unfaithfulness, and Whose almighty Spirit can enable us to perform all Gospel obedience for the time to come.

I find much comfort, in my weak state of health, from my relation to my *Covenant God*. By my relation to Him as my

Covenant God I mean (1) My clear, explicit knowledge of the Father as my Creator and Father, Who so loved the world—you and me—as to give His only begotten Son, that we should not perish but have everlasting life. O! my dear friends, what sweet exclamations, what endearing calling of "Abba Father" will ascend from our grateful hearts if we say with St. Paul, "He that spared not His own Son, but delivered Him up for us all, how freely will He give us all things" with that capital Gift?

(2) I mean by my covenant relation, my relation to the adorable Person Who, with the strength of His Godhead and the strength of His pure manhood, took away my sin and reconciled our fallen race to the divine nature, making us capable of recovering the divine union from which Adam fell. O how does my soul exult in that dear Mediator! How do I hide my poor soul under the shadow of His wings! There let me meet you all. Driven to that true mercy seat by the same danger, drawn by the same preserving and redeeming love; invited by the same gospel promises, and encouraged by each others example and by the example of that cloud of witnesses who have passed into the Kingdom of God by that precious door, let us by Christ return to God. Let us in Christ find our reconciled God. And may that dear commandment of His, "Abide in Me," prove every day more precious to our souls. If we abide in Him by believing that He is our way, our truth, and our life—by apprehending Him as our Prophet or wisdom, our Priest or righteousness, our King or sanctification and redemption—we shall bear fruit. And we shall understand what is meant by these Scriptures, "In Him I am well pleased;" "Accepted in the beloved;" "There is no condemnation to them that are in Christ Jesus;" "God was in Christ reconciling the world unto Himself;" etc.

O the comfort of cleaving to Christ by faith and of finding that Christ is our all! In that center of life let us all meet, and death itself will not separate us; for Christ, our Life, is the Resurrection. And Christ, our common Resurrection, will bring us back from the grave to worship Him altogether, where absence and sickness shall interrupt and separate us no more.

I sometimes feel a desire of being buried where you are buried, and having my bones lie in a common earthen bed with yours. I soon resign that wish, however, and, leaving that particular to Providence, I exult in thinking that whatever distance there may be between our graves, we can now bury our sins, cares, doubts, and fears in the one grave of our divine Savior. We may rejoice, each of us in our measure, that neither life nor death, neither things present nor things to come, shall ever be able (while we hang on the Crucified as He hung on the cross) to separate us from Christ our Head, nor from the love of each other, His members.

I entreat you then, my dear brethren, love one another... If I, your poor, unworthy shepherd am smitten, be not scattered. On the contrary, be more closely gathered into Christ. Keep near each other in faith and love till you all receive our second Comforter and Advocate in the glory of His fullness... This indwelling of the Comforter perfects the mystery of sanctification in the believer's soul. This is the highest blessing of the Christian covenant on earth. Rejoicing in God our Creator, in God our Redeemer, let us look for the full comfort of God our Sanctifier...

My paper fails, but not my love. It embraces you all in the bowels of Jesus Christ, to whose love I earnestly recommend you. I earnestly desire you would recommend to His faithful mercy your affectionate friend and brother, your unworthy pastor and fellow-helper in the faith.

To William Wase

Newington, Jan. 13th, 1777

My Dear Brother—I am two kind letters in your debt. I would have answered them before, but I ventured to ride out in the frost, and the air was too sharp for my weak lungs, and opened my wound, which has thrown me back again.

I am glad to see by your last that you take up your shield again. You will never prove a gainer by vilely casting it away. Voluntary humility, despondency, or even a defeat should not make you give up your confidence, but rather make you hug your shield and embrace your Savior with redoubled ardor and courage. To whom should you go, but to Him Who hath the words of everlasting life? And if you give up your faith, do you not block up the way by which you should return to Him? Let it be the last time you compliment the enemy with what you should fight for to the last drop of your blood.

You must not be above being employed in a little way. The great Mr. Grimshaw was not above walking some miles to preach to seven or eight people, and what are we compared to him? Our neighborhood will want you more when Mr. Greaves and I are gone. In the mean time, grow in meek, humble, patient, resigned love; and your temper, person, and labors will be more acceptable to all around you. I have many things to say to you about your soul, but you will find the substance of them in two sermons of Mr. Wesley's. One is entitled "The Devices of Satan," and the other is "The Repentance of Believers." I wish you would read one of them every day till you have reaped all the benefit that can be got from them. And do not eat your morsel alone, but let all be benefited by the contents. I am, etc.

To Miss Perronet

Newington, Jan. 19th, 1777

Dear Madam—I thank you for your care and kind nursing of me when at Shoreham, and especially for the few lines you have favored me with. They are so much the more agreeable to me as they treat of the one thing needful for the recovery of our souls—the spirit of power, of love, and of a sound mind, together with our need of it, and the grand promise that this need shall be abundantly supplied—supplied by a baptismal outpouring of that Spirit of life in Christ Jesus which makes us free from the law of sin and death. May we hunger and thirst after righteousness in the Holy Ghost, and we shall be filled. May we so come to our first Paraclete, Advocate, and Comforter as to receive the Second as an indwelling and overflowing fountain of light, life, and love.

My view of this mystery is, I trust, Scriptural. The Father so loved the world as to give us the first Advocate, Paraclete, and Comforter, Whom we love and receive as our Redeemer. The first Advocate has told us it was expedient that He should leave us, because in that case He would send another Advocate, Paraclete, or Comforter, to abide with us and be in us for ever as our Sanctifier, our Urim and Thummim, our lights and perfections, our oracle and guide. This is the grand promise to Christians—called the promise of the Father and brought by the Son. O may it be sealed on our hearts by the Spirit of promise! May we ever cry

Seal thou our breasts, and let us wear
That pledge of love for ever there!

Then we shall be filled with pure, perfect love; for the love of the Spirit perfects that of the Father and Son, and accomplishes the mystery of God in the believing soul. Come then, let us look for it. This great salvation draws nigh. Let us thank God more thankfully, more joyfully, more humbly, more penitently, for Christ our first Comforter. And then, hanging on His word, let us ardently pray for the fullness of His Spirit, for the indwelling of our second Comforter, Who will lead us into all truth, all love, all power. Let us join the few who besiege the throne of grace, and not give over putting the Lord in remembrance till He has raised Himself a Pentecostal Church again in the earth. I mean a Church of such believers as are all of one heart and one soul. Nor forget to ask that, when you press into that Kingdom and Church, you may be followed by, Dear Madam, Yours, etc.

TO JAMES IRELAND

Newington, Jan. 29th, 1777

MY DEAR FRIEND— ... Last Sunday, Providence sent me Dr. Turner, who, under God, saved my life twenty-three years ago in a dangerous illness. I am inclined to try what his method will do. He orders me asses' milk, chicken, etc., forbids me riding, and recommends the greatest quietness. He prohibits the use of Bristol water, advises some waters of a purgative nature, and tries to promote expectoration by a method that so far answers, though I spit by it more blood than before. It will be in order to cure one way or other.

With respect to my soul, I find it good to be in the balance, awfully weighed every day for life or death. I thank God that the latter has lost its sting and endears to me the Prince of Life. But O! I want Christ my Resurrection to be a thousand times more dear to me, and I doubt not He will be so when I am *filled* with the Spirit of wisdom and revelation in the knowledge of Him. Let us wait for that glory, praising God for all we have received and do daily receive, and trusting Him for all we have not yet received. Let our faith do justice to His veracity, our hope to His goodness, and our love to all His perfections. It is good to trust in the Lord, and His saints like well to hope in Him.

I am provided here with every necessary and convenient blessing for my state. The great have even done me the honor of calling—Mr. Shirley, Mr. R——d Hill, Mr. Peckwell, etc. I exhort them to promote peace in the Church, which they take kindly. I hope God will incline us all to peace, living and dying. Lady Huntingdon has written me a kind letter also. O for universal, lasting kindness! This world to me is now become a world of love. May it be so to my dear friend also. My kindest love and thanks wait on yourself, Mrs. Ireland, and all your dear family.

To Mr. Greenwood

London, 1777

My Dear Companion in tribulation, and in the patience of Jesus. Peace be multiplied unto you, and resignation by the cross of Jesus. I bear your foot on my heart, and cast my heart on Him to Whom all burdens are lighter than a feather. Paschal said, when the rod of tribulation was upon him, "Now I begin to be a Christian," meaning a follower of the Man of Sorrows. By His pierced feet may yours be eased. Hold this fast: "Whom the Lord loveth, He chasteneth." Accept the rod as a token of your adoption, and be willing to be made perfect in patience by *sufferings*. In the mean time rejoice that Christ's sufferings are over—that they are *atoning*—and that they have *purchased* our comforts. If you can come safely tomorrow, you will bring a blessing to your poor pensioner, who remains in the bonds of grateful, brotherly love, yours.

To James Ireland

Newington, Feb. 24th, 1777

My Dear Friend—Let us abandon ourselves without reserve to God, who is alike the God of all grace when He chastises as when He blesses us. Be a son of Abraham—be an imitator of God. Abraham refused not to offer up his Isaac, and God has delivered His only Son to death for us. Refuse nothing to this God of love and tender compassion. The sacrifice of those things which are most precious to us are the least unworthy of Him. Had we a thousand Isaacs, we ought to keep back none from Him. Perhaps the Lord hath heard your prayer and ours. If your Isaac lives, may he be devoted to the Lord as was Samuel, and may the God of Elijah have all the glory of his recovery. If he be dead, prepare to follow him, and do not envy him the sweet repose which he enjoys, and in which we shall soon share with him.

Adieu. They forbid my writing, but I will write to the last, "Blessed be God Who giveth us the victory over death and its pains by Jesus Christ!" In Him I am, and shall always be altogether yours. I am your ten thousand times obliged friend.

PS. Your second letter, which reached me when the above was written, informs me of your loss. But why should I call God's securing your son and giving him eternal life your loss? It is Christ's gain Who sees in that sweet child the travel of his childhood; and it is your son's gain, since his conflicts and dangers are now over, and nothing awaits him but an eternal increase of happiness. Who knows but what God, Who foresees all the storms of corruption and rocks of sin we are likely to meet with in the sea of life, has taken your dear child at the best, and by this premature death secures him from eternal death? Come, then, do not repine. God has made you the instrument of adding one more little cherub to the heavenly host, and in this light you may well say, "The Lord gave, and the Lord hath taken away, and blessed be the name of the Lord!" He is better than ten sons. Your son is in His bosom, and this new cord should now draw you from earth to Heaven with a fresh degree of power—with an irresistible attraction.

I thank you ten thousand times over for all your repeated marks of love and generosity to me and mine. The burden is too great to bear. I must cast it upon Him Who can bless you ten thousand times over, and turn all your seeming losses into the greatest blessings. May the God of all consolation help you to reap the earliest and ripest fruit of the affliction whereby He gives you a new token of adoption. Remember my kind love and present my best thanks to Mrs. Ireland.

To Miss Perronet

Newington, April 21st, 1777

My Dear Friend—A thousand thanks to you for your kind, comfortable lines. The prospect of going to see Jesus and His glorified members, and among them your dear departed brother, my now *everliving friend*—this sweet prospect is enough to make me quietly and joyfully submit to leave all my Shoreham friends, and all the excellent ones of the earth. But why do I talk of going to leave any of Christ's members by going to be more intimately united to the Head?

> We all are one, who Him receive,
> And each with each agree;
> In Him the *One*, the *Truth* we live,
> Blest point of unity!

A point this, which fills Heaven and earth—which runs through time and eternity. What an immense point! In it sickness is lost in health, and death in life. There let us ever meet. There to live is Christ, and to die gain…

Give my duty to your father. I throw myself in spirit at his feet, asking his blessing and an interest in his prayers. Tell him that the Lord is gracious to me, does not suffer the enemy to disturb my peace and gives me, in prospect, the victory over death. Thanks be to God, Who giveth us the victory, through our Lord Jesus Christ. Absolute resignation to the Divine Will baffles a thousand temptations, and confidence in our Savior carries us sweetly through a thousand trials. God fill us abundantly with both! …

May our kindred spirits drink deeper into God, till they are filled with all the fullness which our enlarged souls can admit… Let us all tend to our original center and experience that life and death are ours because the Prince of life, Who is our resurrection and life, has overcome sin, death, and the grave for you and for your obliged, unworthy servant.

To Mr. and Mrs. Greenwood

Brislington, May 28th, 1777

My very dear Friends and Benefactors—My prayers shall always be that the merciful may find mercy, and that the great kindness I have found under your quiet roof may be showed you every where under the canopy of Heaven. I think with grateful joy on the days of calm retreat I have been blessed with at Newington and lament my not having improved better the opportunity of sitting, like Mary, at the feet of my great Physician.

May He requite your kind care to a dying worm by abundantly caring for you and yours and making all your bed in your sickness! May you enjoy full health! May you hunger and thirst after righteousness—both that of Christ, and that of the Holy Ghost—and be abundantly filled therewith! May His rod and staff comfort you under all the troubles of life, the decays of the body, the assaults of the enemy, and the pangs of death! May the reviving cordials of the Word of Truth be ever within the reach of your faith; and may your eager faith make a ready and constant use of them, especially when faintings come upon you and your hands begin to hang down! May you stand in the clefts of the Rock of Ages, and there be safely sheltered when all the storms of justice shall fall around! May you have always such temporal and spiritual helps, friends, and comforts as I have found in your pleasing retreat!

You have received a poor Lazarus, though his sores were not visible. You have had compassion like the good Samaritan. You have admitted me to the enjoyment of your best things; and he that did not deserve to have the dogs to lick his sores has always found the members of Jesus ready to prevent, to remove, or to bear his burdens. And now what shall I say? "Thanks be unto God for His unspeakable gift!" And thanks to my dear friends for all their favors! They will, I trust, be found faithfully recorded in my breast when the great Rewarder of those who diligently seek Him will render to every man according to his works. Then shall a raised Lazarus appear in the gate to testify of the love of Charles and Mary Greenwood and of their godly sister.

I thought myself a little better last Sunday, but I have since spit more blood than I had done for weeks before. Glory be to God for every providence! His will be done in me by health or sickness, by life or death! All from Him is, and I trust will always be, welcome to your obliged pensioner.

To Vincent Perronet

Sept. 6th, 1777

My Very Dear Father—I humbly thank you for the honor and consolation of your two kind letters. Your vouchsafing to remember a poor, unprofitable worm is to me a sure token that my heavenly Father earnestly remembers me still. He is God—therefore I am not consumed. He is a merciful, all-gracious God—therefore I am blessed with sympathizing friends and gracious helpers on all sides. O sir, if in this disordered, imperfect state of the Church I meet with so much kindness, what shall I not meet with when the millennium you pray for shall begin? O that the thought, the glorious hope, may animate me to perfect holiness in the fear of God, that I may be accounted worthy to escape the terrible judgments which will make way for that happy state of things, and that I may have a part in the first resurrection, if I am numbered among the dead before that happy period begin!

O for a firm and lasting faith,
To credit all the Almighty saith!
To embrace the promise of His Son,
And call that glorious Rest our own!

We are saved by hope at this time; but hope that is seen is not hope. Let us abound then in hope through the power of the Holy Ghost; for so shall we antedate the millennium, take the Kingdom, and enjoy beforehand the rest which remains for the people of God. Your great age, dear sir, and my great weakness have brought us to the verge of eternity. O! may we exult in the prospect. May we look on that boundless sea through the glass of faith and through the clefts of the Rock of Ages, struck for us through the veil of Christ's flesh, Who, by dying for our sins and rising again for our justification, is become our Resurrection and our Life.

Last week one of my parishioners brought a horse to carry me home and desired to walk by my side all the way. By the advice of your dear son, William, who still continues to bestow upon me all the help I could expect from the most loving brother, I sent the man back.

I thank God that I am a little stronger than when I came hither. I kiss the rod, lean on the staff, and wait the end. I yesterday saw a physician who told me my case is not yet an absolutely lost case. But the prospect of languishing two or three years longer, a burden to every body, an help to none, would be very painful, if the will of God and the covenant of life in Christ Jesus did not sanctify all circumstances and dispel every gloom. I remember with grateful joy the happy days I spent at Shoreham. But, what is better still, I shall live with the Lord and with you for ever and ever. I am your obliged servant and affectionate son.

To Mrs. Thornton

Brislington, 1777

My Very Dear Friend—I hope these lines will find you leaving the things that are behind and pressing forward toward the mark—the prize of our high calling on earth. In Heaven we are called to be filled with all we can hold of the glorious fullness of God. What that is we know not, but we shall know, if we follow on to know the Lord. But here also we are called to be filled with all the fullness of God. God is love you know. To be filled with all His fullness is, then, to be filled with love. O may that love be shed abroad in our hearts by the Holy Ghost given to us and abiding in us! I still look for that ineffable fullness. And I beg you, if you have not yet attained it, you would let nothing damp your hope, and slack your pursuit…

I am going to do by my poor sister what you have done by me—I mean, try to smooth the road of sickness to the chamber of death. Gratitude and blood call me to it—you have done it without such calls. Your brotherly kindness is freer than mine; but not so free as the love of Jesus, Who took upon Him our nature, that He might bear our infirmities, die our death, and make over to us His resurrection and His life, after all we had done to render *life hateful* and *death horrible* to Him. O! for this matchless love. Let rocks and hills, let hearts and tongues break an ungrateful silence. Let your Christian muse find new anthems, and your poetic heart new flights of eloquence and thankfulness. You partly owe me, by promise, a piece of poetry on joy in redeeming and sanctifying love. May the spirit of praise assist you mightily in the noble work! Maintain the frame of poetic Christian joy by using all your talents of grace and nature to embrace and show forth His goodness.

I shall be glad to hear from you in Switzerland, and shall doubly rejoice if you can send me word that she who is joined to the Lord according to the glory of the new covenant is one spirit with Him, and enjoys all the glorious liberty of the children of God. The God of peace be with you all!

To the Right Hon. Lady Mary Fitzgerald

Madeley, Oct. 21st, 1777

Honored and Dear Madam—The honor of your Christian letter humbles me, and the idea of your taking half a dozen steps, much more that of your taking a journey to consult so mean a creature, lays me in the dust. My brothers and sisters invite me to breathe once more my natal air, and the physicians recommend to me a journey to the Continent. I wait for the last intimations of Providence to determine me to go. If I do, I shall probably pass through London. In that case, I could have the honor of waiting upon you…

With respect to the hints you drop in your letter concerning your *external* circumstances, I find it upon my heart to say: Abide in the state in which you have been called, till Providence makes a way for you to escape out of what may be contrary to your new taste. Your cross has changed its nature with your heart; and we may, in some cases, be called to take up a worldly as well as a heavenly cross. Joseph and Moses did so once in Egypt, Esther in Susa, Daniel in Babylon, John the Baptist at Herod's court, and our Lord in the house of the rich Pharisee. Some great end, to yourself or to others, may be answered by patiently bearing your worldly cross till it be taken from you, or you are removed from under it. Continue to make it matter of earnest prayer to know the will of God concerning you. And whilst your eye watches the motions of the providential cloud, and your heart listens for the Lord's call, endeavor to keep your will as an even balance at His feet, that the least grain of intimation—clear intimation from Him—and the least distinct touch of the hand of Providence, may turn the scale either way, without resistance on your part. Being thus fully persuaded you will do and suffer all with the liberty and courage of faith.

You have been afflicted as well as dear Mrs. G——, Mrs. L——, and myself. May our maladies yield the peaceable fruits of righteousness—complete deadness to the world and increased faith in the mercy, love, and power of Him Who supports under the greatest trials and can make our extremity of weakness an opportunity of displaying the freeness of His grace and the greatness of His power. Tell Mrs. G—— and Mrs. L—— that I salute them under the cross with the sympathy of a companion in tribulation, and rejoice at the thought of doing it when the cross shall be exchanged for the crown. In the meantime let us glory in the cross of our common Head, and firmly believe that He is exalted to give us whatever is best for us in life, in death, and for ever…

In order to live singly to God, the best method is to desire it with meekness; to spread the desire in quietness before Him Who inspired it; to offer Him now all we have and are, as we can; and to enlarge our expectation that He may satisfy it with good things, with all His fullness, or that He may try our patience and teach us to know our total helplessness. With respect to the weeping frame of repentance and the joyous one of faith, they are both good alternately; but the latter is the better of the two, because it enables us to do and suffer the will of God, and praise Him, which honors Christ more. Both are happily mixed. May they be so in you, Madam, and in your unworthy and obliged servant.

To Mr. William Wase

Bristol, Nov. 1777

My Dear Brother—Pardon the trouble I have given you in my temporal concerns, although it is more for the poor and the Lord than for me. O! my dear friend, let us pass through the things temporal so as not to lose the things eternal. Let us honor God's truth by believing His Word and Christ's blood; by hoping firmly in divine mercy, and all the divine perfections; by loving God with all our hearts, and one another as Christ loved us. My kind love to all the brethren on both sides the water.

Go from me to Mrs. Cound. Tell her that I charge her in the name of God to give up the world, to set out with all speed for Heaven, and to join the few that fear God about her. If she refuse, call weekly, if not daily, and warn her from me. Tell the brethren at Broseley that I did my body an injury the last time I preached to them on the green; but I do not repine at it if they took the warning and have ceased to be neither hot nor cold and begin to be warm in zeal, love, prayer, and every grace. Give my love to George Crannage. Tell him to make haste to Christ and not to doze away his last days.

The physician has not yet given me up; but I bless God that I do not wait for his farewell to give myself up to my God and Savior. I write by stealth, as my friends here would have me forbear writing and even talking. But I will never part with my privileges of writing and shouting, "Thanks be to God, who giveth us the victory" over sin, death, and the grave, "through Jesus Christ!" To Him be glory for ever and ever.

To the Brethren at the Parish Church of Madeley

Bristol, Nov. 26th, 1777

My Dear Brethren—I thank you for the declaration of your affectionate remembrance which you have sent me by John

Owen, the messenger of your brotherly love. As a variety of reasons (with which I shall not trouble you) prevent my coming to take my leave of you in person, permit me to do it by letter. The hopes of recovering a little strength to come and serve you again in the Gospel make me take the advice of the physicians, who say that removing to a drier air and warmer climate might be of great service to my health. I kiss the rod which smites me. I adore the Providence which lays me aside, and beg that by this long correction of my heavenly Father, I may be so pruned as to bring forth more fruit, if I am spared.

I am more and more persuaded that I have not declared unto you cunningly devised fables, and that the Gospel I have had the honor of preaching, though feebly, among you, is the power of God to salvation to every one who believes it with the heart. God grant we may all be of that happy number.

Want of time does not permit me to give you more directions, but if you follow those which fill the rest of this page, they may supply the want of a thousand.

Have, every day, lower thoughts of yourselves, higher thoughts of Christ, kinder thoughts of your brethren, and more hopeful thoughts of all around you. Love to assemble in the great congregation and with your companions in tribulation. Above all, love to pray to your Father in secret; to consider your Savior, Who says, "Look unto me and be saved;" to listen for your Sanctifier and Comforter, Who whispers that He stands at the door and knocks to enter into your inmost souls that He might set up His Kingdom of righteousness, peace, and joy, with divine power, in your willing breasts. Wait all the day long for His glorious appearing within you. When you are together, by suitable prayers, proper hymns, and enlivening exhortations, keep up your earnest expectation of His pardoning and sanctifying love.

Let not a drop satisfy you—desire an ocean, or at least a fountain springing up to your comfort in your own souls, and flowing towards all around you in streams of love and delightful instructions, to the consolation of those with whom you converse—especially your brethren and those of your own households. Do not eat your morsel by yourselves, like selfish, niggardly people. Whether you eat the meat that perisheth, or that which endureth unto everlasting life, be ready to share it with all. Cast your bread upon the waters, in a temporal or spiritual sense, and it will not be lost. God will bless your seed sown, and it will abundantly increase.

Let every one with whom you converse be the better for your conversation. Be burning and shining lights wherever you are. Set the fire of divine love to the hellish stubble of sin. Be valiant for the truth. Be champions for love. Be sons of thunder against sin, and sons of consolation towards humbled sinners. Be faithful to your God, your king, and your masters. Let not the good ways of God be blasphemed through any of you. Let your heavenly-mindedness and your brotherly-kindness be known to all men, so that all who see you may wonder, and say, "See how these people love one another!"

You have need of patience, as well as of faith and power. You must learn to suffer as well as to do the will of God. Do not, then, think it strange to pass through fiery trials—they are excellent for the proving, purifying, and strengthening of your faith. Only let your faith be firm in a tempest. Let your hope in Christ be as a sure anchor cast within the veil, and your patient love will soon outride the storm and make you find that there is a peace in Christ and in the Holy Ghost which no man can give or take away. May that peace be abundantly given to you from our common Father, our common Redeemer, and our common Sanctifier, our Covenant God, Whom we have so often vouched to be our God and our All when we have been assembled together in His Name. He is the same merciful and faithful God, yesterday, today, and for ever. Believe in His threefold name. Rejoice in every degree of His great salvation. Triumph in the hope of the glory which shall be revealed. Do not forget to be thankful for a cup of water—much less for being out of hell, for the means of grace, the forgiveness of sins, the blood of Jesus, the communion of saints on earth, and the future glorification of saints in heaven. Strongly, heartily believe every gospel truth, especially the latter part of the apostles' creed. Believe it, I say, till your faith becomes to you the substance of the eternal Life you hope for. And then, come life, come death—either or both will be welcome to you as, through grace, I find they are to me.

I leave this blessed Island for a while; but I trust I shall never leave the Kingdom of God, the Mount Sion, the New Jerusalem, the shadow of Christ's cross, the clefts of the Rock smitten and pierced for us. There I entreat you to meet me. There I meet you in spirit. From thence I trust I shall joyfully leap into the ocean of eternity to go and join those ministering spirits who wait on the heirs of salvation. If I am no more permitted to minister to you in the land of the living, I rejoice at the thought that I shall, perhaps, be allowed to accompany the angels, who, if you continue in the faith, will be commissioned to carry your souls into Abraham's bosom. If our bodies do not molder away in the same grave, our spirits shall be sweetly lost in the same sea of divine and brotherly love. I hope to see you again in the flesh; but my sweetest and firmest hope is to meet you where there are no parting seas, no interposing mountains, no sickness, no death, no fear of loving too much, no shame for loving too little, no apprehension of bursting new vessels in our lungs by indulging the joy of seeing or the sorrow of leaving our brethren.

In the mean time, I earnestly recommend you to the pastoral care of the Great Shepherd and Bishop of souls and to the brotherly care of one another, as well as to the ministerial care of my substitute. The authority of love, which you allowed me to exert among you for edification, I return to you and divide among you, humbly requesting that you would mutually use it in warning the unruly, supporting the weak, and comforting all. Should I be spared to come back, let me have the joy of finding you all of one heart and one soul, continuing steadfast in the Apostle's doctrine, in fellowship one with another, and in communion with our sin-pardoning and sin-abhorring God. This you may do through grace, by strongly believing in the atoning blood and sanctifying Spirit of Christ, our common Head and our common Life, in Whom my soul embraces you, and in Whose gracious hands I leave both you and myself. Bear me on your hearts before Him in praying love; and be persuaded that you are thus borne by, my dear brethren, yours, etc.

To Miss Perronet

Reading, Dec. 2nd, 1777

My Dear Friend—I snatch a moment upon the road to acknowledge the favor of your letter, and to wish you joy in seeing that the Lord is faithful in rewarding as well as punishing. I once met a gentleman abroad, an infidel, who said, "Men have no faith. If they believed that by forsaking houses, lands, friends, etc., they should receive an hundredfold, they would instantly renounce all. For who would not carry all his money to the bank of Heaven to receive an hundredfold interest?"

The Papists have made so bad a use of the rewardableness of works that we dare neither preach it nor hold it in a Scriptural manner. For my part, I think that if it were properly received, it would make a great alteration in the professing world. Dare to receive it! Try the mighty use of it! Then, when you have fully experienced it, do not keep your light to yourself, but impart it to all within the reach of your tongue and pen. I am glad you see that, after all, every reward bestowed upon a reprieved sinner has free grace for its foundation and the blood of Christ for its mark. May the richest rewards of divine grace be yours, in consequence of the most exalted faithfulness. Let me beseech you to pray that I may follow you as you follow Christ, till our reward be full. That God may fill you with all His fullness is the wish of, my dear friend, your obliged brother.

To the Societies in and about Madeley

Nyon, 1778

My Dear, Very Dear Brethren—This comes with my best love to you and my best wishes that peace, mercy, and truth may be multiplied unto you from God the Father, through Jesus Christ, by the Spirit of His love. And I beg that your hearts and mine may be daily more replenished with this love.

I am yet in the land of the living to prepare, with you, for the land where there is life without death, praising without weariness of the flesh, and loving without separation. *THERE* I once more challenge you to meet me with all the mind that was in Christ. And may not one hoof be left behind! May there not be found one Demas amongst you, turning aside from the little flock and the narrow way to love and follow this present perishing world. May there not be one Esau, who, for a frivolous gratification sold his birthright; nor another wife of Lot, who looked back for the good things of the city of destruction, and was punished by a judgment almost as fearful as that of Ananias, Sapphira, and Judas.

My dear companions, let us be consistent. Let us seek first the Kingdom of God and His righteousness; and then all other things, upon your *diligent*, *frugal*, *secondary* endeavors, shall be added unto you. Let us live daily, more and more, upon the free love of our gracious Creator and Preserver, the grace and righteousness of our atoning Redeemer and Mediator, nor let us stop short of the powerful, joyous influence of our Comforter and Sanctifier.

Bear me on your hearts, as I do you upon mine. Let us all meet in the heart of Christ, Who is the center of our union and our common Head, humbly leaving it to Him *when* and *where* we shall meet again. In the mean while I beg you will pay a due regard to the following texts: "Love one another, as I have loved you." "By this shall all men know that ye are my disciples, if ye love one another." "Little children, love not the world; for if any man love the world, the love of the Father, and of the brethren, is not in him." "Be of one accord, of one mind." "Let there be no divisions among you." "Mind not high things," but things which make for peace and edification.

Farewell in Christ till we meet in the flesh around His table, or in the spirit around His Throne. I am your afflicted, comforted brother.

To John and Charles Wesley

Macon, May 17th, 1778

Rev. and Dear Sirs—I hope that while I lie by like a broken vessel, the Lord continues to renew your vigor, and sends you to water His vineyard and to stand in the gap against error and vice. I have recovered some strength, blessed be God, since I came to the Continent, but have lately had another attack of my old complaints. However, I find myself better again, though I think it yet advisable not to speak in public.

I preached twice at Marseilles, but was not permitted to follow the blow. There are few noble, inquisitive Bereans in these parts. The ministers in the town of my nativity have been very civil. They have offered me the pulpit, but I fear if I could accept the offer it would soon be recalled. I am loath to quit this part of the field without casting a stone at that giant, Sin, who stalks about with uncommon boldness. I shall, therefore, stay some months longer to see if the Lord will please to give me a little more strength to venture an attack.

Gaming and dress, sinful pleasure and love of money, unbelief and false philosophy, lightness of spirit, fear of man, and love of the world are the principal sins by which Satan binds his captives in these parts. Materialism is not rare. Deism and Socinianism are very common. And a set of freethinkers, great admirers of Voltaire and Rosseau, Bayle and Mirabeau, seem bent upon destroying Christianity and government. "With one hand (said a lawyer who has written something against them) they shake the throne, and with the other they throw down the altars." If we believe them, the world is the dupe of kings and priests. Religion is fanaticism and superstition. Subordination is slavery and tyranny. Christian morality is absurd, unnatural, and impracticable. Christianity is the most bloody religion that ever was. And here it is certain that by the example of *so called* Christians, and by our continual disputes, they have a great advantage, and do the truth immense mischief. Popery will certainly fall in France, in this or the next century. And I make no doubt that God will use those vain men to bring about a reformation here, as he used Henry the Eighth to do that work in England. So the madness of His enemies shall, at last, turn to His praise and to the furtherance of His Kingdom.

In the mean time it becomes all lovers of the truth to make their heavenly tempers and humble, peaceful love to shine before all men, that those mighty adversaries, seeing the good works of professors, may glorify their Father Who is in Heaven, and no more blaspheme that worthy name by which we are all called Christians.

If you ask, "What system do these men adopt?" I answer that some build on Deism—a morality founded on self-preservation, self-interest, and self-honor. Others laugh at all morality except that which, being neglected, violently disturbs society; and external order is the decent covering of Fatalism, while Materialism is their system.

O dear sirs, let me entreat you in these dangerous days to use your wide influence, with unabated zeal, against the scheme of these modern Celsuses, Porphiries, and Julians. Do this by calling all professors to think and speak the same things, to love and embrace one another, and to stand firmly embodied to resist those daring men, many of whom are already in England headed by the admirers of Mr. Hume and Mr. Hobbes. But it is needless to say this to those who have made and continue to make such a stand for vital Christianity; so that I have nothing to do but to pray that the Lord would abundantly support and strengthen you to the last, and make you a continued comfort to His enlightened people, loving reprovers of those who mix light and darkness, and a terror to the perverse. This is the cordial prayer of, Rev. and dear Sirs, your affectionate son and obliged servant in the Gospel.

PS. I need not tell you, Sirs, that the hour in which Providence shall make my way plain to return to England to unite with the happy number of those who feel or seek the power of Christian godliness will be welcome to me. O favored Britons! Happy would it be for them if they knew their Gospel privileges! My relations in Adam are all very kind to me. But the spiritual relations whom God has raised me in England exceed them yet. Thanks be to Christ and to His blasphemed religion!

To Dr. Conyers

Macon, May 18th, 1778

Dear Sir— … If you saw with what boldness the false philosophers of the Continent, who are the apostles of the age, attack Christianity and represent it as one of the worst religions in the world—fit only to make the professors of it murder one another, or at least to contend among themselves; if you saw how they urge our disputes that they may make the Gospel of Christ the jest of nations and the abhorrence of all flesh, you would break through your natural timidity and invite all our brethren in the ministry to do what the herds do on the Swiss mountains when the wolves attack them. Instead of goring one another, they unite, form a close battalion, and face the common enemy on all sides. What a shame would it be if cows and bulls showed more prudence and more regard for union than Christians and Gospel Ministers! …

To his Curate, Mr. Greaves

My Very Dear Brother—I am in daily expectation of a line from you to let me know how you do, and how it goes with our dear flock… O my dear brother, no religion will, in the end, do us and our people any good, but that which "works by love"—humble, childlike, obedient love. May that religion fill our souls and influence all our tempers, words, and actions… May St. James's peaceable religion spread through all our parish. Please, at the first convenient opportunity, read the following note in the church.

"John Fletcher sends his best Christian love to the congregation that worships God in the Parish Church at Madeley.

He begs the continuance of their prayers for strength of body and mind, that he may be able, if it be the will of God, to serve them again in the Gospel. He desires them to return Almighty God thanks for having enabled him to speak again in public last Sunday without having had a return of his spitting of blood, which he considers as a token that his life may be spared a little to go and exhort them to grow in grace, in the knowledge of our Lord Jesus Christ, and in brotherly love—the best marks that we know God and are in the faith of Christ."

I hope, my dear brother, you are settled to your satisfaction. I shall be glad to do what is in my power to make your stay at Madeley agreeable. I hope you read sometimes in the study the copy of the exhortation given us by the Ordinary, in which are these awful words: "Cease not from your labor, care, and diligence, till all those who are committed to your charge come to such a ripeness of age in Christ that there be no room left among them for error in doctrine or viciousness in life." I wish you may have as much success as we desire. But whatever success we have, we must cast our bread upon the waters, though we should see as little fruit as he that said of old, "I have labored in vain." Our reward will be with the Lord if not with men.

To Mr. William Perronet

Nyon, June 2nd, 1778

My Dear Friend— ...While I write to you to make your title clear to a precarious estate on earth, permit me to remind you of the heavenly inheritance entailed upon believers. The Will (the New Testament) by which we can recover it is proved; the Court is equitable; the Judge is loving and gracious. To enter on the possession of part of the estate here and of the whole hereafter, we need only to believe, and to prove *evangelically* that we are believers. Let us set about it now with earnestness, with perseverance, and with full assurance that through faith we shall infallibly carry our cause. Alas! what are estates or crowns compared to grace and glory? The Lord grant that we and all our friends may choose the better part, which your brother, my dear friend, so happily chose. And may we firmly stand to the choice to the last, as he did. My best respects wait upon your dear father, your sisters, and your nieces. God reward your kindness to me upon them all! …

This is a delightful country. If you come to see it and claim the estate, bring all the papers and memorials your father can collect. Come and share a pleasant apartment and one of the finest prospects in the world in the house where I was born. I design to try this fine air some months longer. We have a fine shady wood near the lake, where I can ride in the cool all the day and enjoy the singing of a multitude of birds. But this, though sweet, does not come up to the singing of my dear friends in England. There I meet them in spirit several hours in the day. God bless my dear friends.

To James Ireland

Nyon, July 15th, 1778

My Dear Friend—I have ventured to preach once and to expound once in the church. Our ministers are very kind and preach to the purpose. A young one of this town gave us lately a very excellent Gospel sermon. Grown-up people stand fast in their stupidity, or in their self-righteousness.

The day I preached, I met with some children in my wood walking or gathering strawberries. I spoke to them about our Father… The next day… I inquired after them and invited them to come to me, and this they have done every day since. I make them little hymns which they sing. Some of them are under sweet drawings. Yesterday I wept for joy on hearing one of them speak of conviction of sin and joy unspeakable in Christ which had followed—as an experienced believer would do in Bristol.

Last Sunday I met them in the wood. There were one hundred of them, and as many adults. Our first pastor has since desired me to desist from preaching in the wood for fear of giving umbrage. I have complied with his desire, due to a concurrence of circumstances which are not worth mentioning, and now meet them in my father's yard.

In one of my letters I promised you some anecdotes concerning the death of our two great philosophers, Voltaire and Rousseau. Mr. Tronchin, the physician of the Duke of Orleans, being sent for to attend Voltaire in his illness at Paris, Voltaire said to him, "Sir, I desire you would save my life. I will give you the half of my fortune if you lengthen out my days only for six months. If not, I shall go to the devil and shall carry you away along with me."

Rousseau died more decently, as full of himself as Voltaire was of the wicked one. He paid that attention to nature and the natural sun which the Christian pays to grace and the Sun of Righteousness. The following were some of his last words to his wife, which I copy from a printed letter circulating in these parts: "Open the window that I may see the green fields once more. How beautiful is nature! How wonderful is the sun! See what glorious light it sends forth! It is God Who calls me. How pleasing is death to a man who is not conscious of any sin! O God! my soul is now as pure as when it first came out of Thy hands; crown it with Thy heavenly bliss!"

God deliver us from self and Satan, the internal and external fiend. The Lord forbid we should fall into the snare of the Sadducees with the former of these two famous men, or into that of the Pharisees with the latter. Farewell in Jesus.

To Mr. Greaves

Nyon, July 18th, 1778

My Dear Brother— ... I trust you lay yourself out in length and breadth for the good of the flock committed to your care. I should be glad to hear that all the flock grow in grace, and that the little flock grow in humble love.

Be pleased to read the following note in the church:

> John Fletcher begs a further interest in the prayers of the congregation of Madeley. He desires those who assemble to serve God in the church to help him to return public thanks to Almighty God for many mercies received. Especially is he grateful for being able to do every day a little ministerial duty, which he considers as an earnest of the strength he should be glad to have in order to come back soon and serve his congregation in the Gospel. This he designs to do, please God, in some months. In the meantime, he beseeches them to serve God as Christians, love one another as brethren, neglect no means of grace, and rejoice in all the hopes of glory.

I hope, my dear brother, that you remember my request to you in my letter from Dover, and that you are glad of every possible help to do the people good. The harvest is great, the *laborers* are but comparatively few. Pray the Lord to send more laborers into His harvest. Rejoice when He sends us any who will help us to break up the fallow ground. My love to all our kind neighbors and to the preachers, whom I beg you will thank in my name.

Be pleased, when you have an opportunity, to read the following note to the Societies at Madeley, Dawley, and the Banks:

> I hope you have no need of a line to assure you of the continuance of my brotherly love for you. We are all called to grow in grace and, consequently, in love, which is the greatest of all Christian graces. Your prayers for my soul and body have not been without answer. Blessed be God! Glory be to His rich mercy in Christ, I live yet the life of faith. As to my body, I recover some strength. This rejoices me the more, as I hope a good Providence will make way for my laying it out in inviting you to leave the things which are behind and to press, with earnestness, unity, and patience, towards the mark of our heavenly calling in Christ. God bless you all with all the blessing brought to the church by Christ Jesus and by the other Comforter! Fare ye all well in Jesus. Remember at the Throne of Grace your affectionate brother and servant in Christ.

My love to all our kind neighbors and to the preachers, whom I beg you will thank in my name. Adieu, my dear brother. I am yours in the Lord.

To His Brother, Henry Fletcher

My Dear Brother— ... I cannot but indulge a hope that God will hear my prayers—that He will have some regard to the tears with which I wet this paper—and that, while you are reading these lines, His grace will operate upon your heart. If you did but know how much joy there would be in Heaven for your conversion; if you could but conceive what transports of gratitude would overflow your heart and mine; if you were but sensible how my bowels are moved for you; surely then, without a moment's delay, you would submit to the grace of that Savior Who is even now speaking in your heart.

And can you still hold out, my dear brother? Are you so entire an enemy to your own happiness, so insensible, so hard, as to decline making a full surrender of yourself to God? I will hope better things of you through the grace of our common Savior. O may that grace overwhelm thy heart and melt down all thy hardness! As we are of one blood, let us also be of one heart and one soul. Do not reject, I conjure you, my brotherly counsels and supplications. Do not refuse to come where so much felicity awaits you because pressed to it by a person who is unworthy to bring you the invitation.

We have passed our infancy and our youth beneath the same roof and under the same masters. We have borne the same fatigues and tasted the same pleasures. Why then should we be separated now? Why should they be divided who by nature, habit, and friendship have been so long united?

I have undertaken a journey to the New Jerusalem. O suffer me not to go thither alone! Let neither the fatigues nor the length of the way affright you. We shall be provided, even in the desert, with heavenly manna and streams of living water. God Himself shall go before us as in a pillar of fire. Under the protection of His wings, we may walk without fear through the valley of the shadow of death. Come then, my dear brother! I am most unwilling to leave you behind. Come, support me. Go before me. Encourage me. Show me the way. I feel the want of a faithful companion and Christian friend.

Suffer me to throw myself at your feet, to embrace your knees, and to wash them with the tears which are now streaming from my eyes. I ask no part of your temporal possessions, but I entreat you to seek after an eternal inheritance. I desire neither your gold nor your silver, but I am anxious that you should share my joy. I am solicitous that you should accompany me to "Mount Zion, to the city of the living God." I desire that you should mix in that "innumerable company of angels" who worship there, and be counted in "the general assembly and church of the firstborn."

In short, I am anxious, my dear brother, that you should come with me to have your name written in the book of life, and be made free of that holy city which shall one day descend from God out of Heaven. I have a presentiment that you will, at last, submit to the easy yoke of Christ, and that after you are converted you will strengthen your brethren. Do not tell me again that piety is usually the portion of younger brothers, since I read in the Old Testament that every firstborn male should be consecrated to God in a peculiar manner. Let me rather entreat you to take the advantage of your situation. Be at least as far beyond me in piety as you are in years; and, instead of feeling any jealousy upon this account, my pleasure will be augmented in the great day of our Lord Jesus Christ to see myself placed at your feet.

To James Ireland

Nyon, Sept. 15th, 1778

My Dear Friend—I am just returned from an excursion I made with my brother through the fine vale in the midst of the high hills which divide France from this country. In that vale we found three lakes—one on French ground and two on Swiss. The largest of these is six miles long and two wide. It is the part of the country where industry is most apparent, and where population thrives best. The inhabitants are chiefly woodmen, coopers, watchmakers, and jewelers. They told me they had the best singing and the best preacher in the country. I asked if any sinners were converted under his ministry. They stared and asked what I meant by conversion. When I had explained myself, they said, "We do not live in the time of miracles."

I was better satisfied in passing through a part of the vale which belongs to the King of France. I saw a prodigious concourse of people and supposed they kept a fair, but was agreeably surprised to find three Missionaries who went about as itinerant preachers to help the regular clergy. They were three brothers and had been there some days already, preaching morning and evening.

The evening service opened by what they called a conference. One of the Missionaries took the pulpit and the parish priest proposed questions to him; these he answered at full length and in a very edifying manner. The subject was the unlawfulness and the mischief of those methods by which persons of different sexes lay snares for each other and corrupt each other's morals. The subject was treated with delicacy, propriety, and truth. The method was admirably well calculated to draw and fix the attention of a mixed multitude. This conference being ended, another missionary took the pulpit. His text was our Lord's description of the day of judgment. Before the sermon, all those who could do so knelt and sung a French hymn to beg a blessing upon the Word; and indeed it was blessed.

An awful attention was visible upon most, and for a good part of the discourse the voice of the preacher was almost lost in the cries and bitter wailings of the audience. When the outcry began, the preacher was describing the departure of the wicked into eternal fire. They urged that God was merciful and that Jesus Christ had shed His blood for them. "But that mercy you have slighted," replies the Judge, "and now is the time of justice. That blood you have trodden under foot, and now it cries for vengeance. Know your day, slight the Father's mercy and the Son's blood no longer." I have seen but once or twice congregations as much affected in England.

One of our Ministers being ill, I ventured a second time into the pulpit last Sunday. The Sunday before, I preached six miles away to 2,000 people in a gaol yard, where they were come to see a poor murderer two days before his execution. I was a little abused by the bailiff on the occasion and refused the liberty of attending the poor man to the scaffold, where he was to be broken on the wheel. I hope he died penitent. The day before he suffered, he said he had broken his irons. As he felt that he deserved to die, however, he desired new ones to be put on, lest he should be tempted to make his escape a second time.

You ask what I design to do. I propose, if it be the Lord's will, to spend the winter here, that I may bear my testimony against the trade of my countrymen.

In the spring I shall, if nothing prevent, return to England with you; or with Mr. Perronet, if his affairs are settled; or alone if other ways fail. In the meantime I rejoice with you in Jesus, and in the glorious hope of that complete salvation which His faithfulness has promised and which His power can never be at a loss to bestow. We must be saved by faith and hope till we are saved by perfect love and made partakers of heavenly glory.

I am truly a stranger here. Well, then, as strangers, let us go where we shall meet the assembly of the righteous gathered in Jesus. Farewell in Him.

To James Ireland

Nyon, Feb. 2nd, 1779

My Dear Friend—I am sorry to hear that you are still tried by illness, but our good heavenly Father will have us to live with one foot on earth and the other in the stirrup of our infirmities, ready to mount and pass from time into eternity. He is wise. His will be done, His name be praised, and our souls saved—though it be by the skin of our teeth!

I am better, thank God, and ride out every day when the slippery roads will permit me to venture without the risk of breaking my horse's legs and my own neck. You will ask me how I have spent my time. I answer: I pray, have patience, rejoice, and write when I can… Several young women seem to have received the Word in the love of it, and four or five more advanced in age; but not one man, except the young hopeful clergyman I mention, who helps me at my little meetings and begins to preach extempore. I hope he will stand his ground better than he who was such an approver when you were here and is now dying after having drawn back to the world.

The truths I chiefly insist upon when I talk to the people who will hear me are those which I feed upon myself as my daily bread. "God, our Maker and Preserver, though invisible, is here and everywhere. He is our chief good, because all beauty and all goodness center in Him and flow from Him. He is especially Love, and love in us, being His image, is the sum and substance of all moral and spiritual excellence, of all true and lasting bliss. In Adam we are all estranged from love and from God. But the Second Adam, Jesus, Emmanuel, God with us, is come to make us know and enjoy again our God, as the God of love and the chief good. All who receive Jesus receive power to become the sons of God, etc., etc."

God bless and comfort you, my dear friend! We are poor creatures, but we have a good God to cast all our burdens upon. He often burdens us so that we may have our constant and free recourse to His bounty, power, and faithfulness. Stand fast in the faith. Believe lovingly, and all will be well. Farewell.

To the Brethren in and about Madeley

Nyon, Feb. 11th, 1779

My Dear Companions in Tribulation—Peace and mercy, faith, hope, and love be multiplied to you all in general, and to each of you in particular, from the Father of mercies, through the Lord Jesus Christ, by the Spirit of grace. I thank you for your kind remembrance of me in your prayers. I am yet spared to pray for you. O that I had more power with God! I would bring down all Heaven into all your hearts. Strive together in love for the living faith, the glorious hope, the sanctifying, perfecting love once delivered to the saints. Look to Jesus. Move on. Run yourselves in the heavenly race, and let each sweetly draw his brother along, till the whole company appears before the Redeeming God in Zion, adorned as a bride for the heavenly Bridegroom.

I hope God will, in His mercy, spare me to see you in the flesh. And if I cannot labor for you, I shall gladly suffer with you. If you will put health into my flesh, marrow in my bones, joy in my heart, and life into my whole frame, be of one heart and of one soul. Count nothing your own but your sin and shame; and bury that dreadful property in the grave, the bottomless grave of our Savior. Let all you are, and have, be His that bought you, and His members, for His sake. Dig hard in the Gospel mines for hidden treasure. Blow hard the furnace of prayer with the bellows of faith, until you are melted into love, and the dross of sin is purged out of every heart. "There is a river that maketh glad the city of God." It is the grace that flows from His throne. Jesus is the vessel, the heavenly ark. Get together into Him, and sweetly sail down into the ocean of eternity. So shall you be true miners, furnace-men, and bargemen. Farewell in Jesus.

To Mr. William Wase

Nyon, Feb. 11th, 1779

My Dear Friend—I have just received yours of the 24th January and rejoice to hear of the welfare of your friends. But there is no blessing here without some alloy of grief, and such was to me the account of the poor state of dear Mrs. Wase's health. The Lord be with her as a *Comforter* and *Sanctifier*, if He does not choose to be with her as a *Physician.* Tell her that I should be glad to hold up her hands in her fight of affliction. But if the poor, unprofitable, weak servant is far off, the Master, Who is rich in mercy, Who fills the whole world with His goodness and patience, and Who has all power given Him as *our brother, Son of Man*, in Heaven and earth: this kind Master is near to her and all His afflicted ones. Bid her from me, entreat her in my name, or rather in His dear name—Jesus, Salvation, Resurrection, Life, Light, and Love—to look to Him, and to make a free and constant use of Him in *all* His offices.

I recommend to her two remedies: the one is a cheerful resignation to the will of God, whereby her animal spirits will be raised and sweetly refreshed. The other is four lumps of heavenly sugar to be taken every half hour, day and night, when she does not sleep. I make a constant use of them to my great comfort. They have quickened my soul when I was dying, and I doubt not but they will have the same effect upon hers. Our Church has already extracted that divine sugar from the Scriptures and put it into the Common Prayer Book, as the heavenly bait which is to draw us to the Lord's table. Though they have often passed through my mouth, when I have called her there, they have lost nothing of their sweetness and force. "God so loved the world, etc." "If any man sin, etc." "It is a faithful saying, etc." "Come unto Me all ye that are weary, etc." God grant her abundance of the faith which rolls these heavenly pills in the mind, and much of that love which sucks their sweetness in the heart. Tell her they go down best if taken in the cup of *thanksgiving*, into which a tear of desire, humility, repentance, or of joy might be dropped occasionally. That tear is to be had by looking simply to Him Who sells oil to the virgins and offered a springing well to the woman of Samaria—Who opened a fountain flowing with heavenly blood and water when He hung for us upon the cross. To Him be praise and glory for ever! Amen!

To Mr. Michael Onions

Nyon, May 18th, 1779

My Dear Brother—I have complied with the request of my friends to stay a little longer, as it was backed by a small society of pious people gathered here. Three weeks ago they got about me and, on their knees, with many tears, besought me to stay till they were a little stronger and able to stand alone. They would not rise till they had got me to comply. Happy would it be for us all if we prayed as earnestly to Him Who can give us *substantial* blessings.

However, yesterday I spoke with a carrier from Geneva, to take me to London, who said he would take us at two week's notice. The Lord is always ready to give our hearts a lift to the Kingdom of grace, through which we must pass to the Kingdom of glory. May we be ready also! The comfort of this journey is that we may all travel together, though our bodies are asunder; for Christ the way is everywhere, and faith in His word is, like His word, one and the same in every age and country. So is holiness the narrow way, for in all places we may love God with all our heart and our neighbor as ourself.

Give my kind love to all who travel in this manner. Invite kindly all who have not yet set out. Stir up earnestly those that loiter, especially Thomas Powis, over whom my heart yearns. Above all, give them the example of leaving the things behind, and pressing towards the mark with renewed vigor. Tell your wife I hold her to her promise of being the Lord's more than ever, because the time is shorter for us both. Tell your mother I expect to find her a bruised reed in herself and a pillar in Christ Jesus. The Lord bless your brother and his wife with that child born, that son given, who shall live to restore to us those whom death carries away… I experience here that kindred in Christ is stronger and dearer than kindred in Adam. Tell Mr. Wase I hope he is a widower in the Lord, devoting himself to the bringing up the Lord's family and his own—both of which require close attendance. My love to your fellow-leaders, and by them to the companies you meet in prayer… Tell them I hope to find them growing up into Christ in all things, particularly in heavenly zeal and humble love. Salute all our dear friends and neighbors for me. Farewell in the Lord.

To Vincent Perronet

May 22nd, 1779

My Very Dear Brother and Honored Father—I rejoice that you are yet preserved to be a witness of Jesus's grace and saving health. Let us rejoice that when our strength shall decay, His will remain entire for ever; and in His strength, we who take Him for our life shall be strong. Our Redeemer liveth. When sickness and death shall have brought down our flesh to the earth, we shall, by His resurrection's power, rise and live for ever with Him in heavenly places. For the new earth will be an Heaven, or a glorious province of the Kingdom of Heaven. With it we shall be restored to paradisiacal beauty and filled with righteousness. The meek shall inherit it, and that inheritance shall be fairer and surer than yours at Chateau d'Oex. I hope to accompany your son soon to England. Let us all move towards our one heavenly country by Christ, Who is the only Way—a Way which is strait, sure, luminous, and where the wayfaring man, though a fool, will have more wisdom than all the teachers of the mere letter.

To Mr. Charles Greenwood

Nyon, May 22nd, 1779

My Dear Friend—I am yet alive, able to ride out, and now and then to instruct a few children. I hope Mr. Perronet will soon have settled his affairs, and then, please God, I shall inform you by word of mouth how much I am indebted to you, Mrs. Greenwood, and Mrs. Thornton. I know it so much the more now, as I have made trial of the kindness of my relations in Adam. Those in Christ exceed them as far, in my account, as grace exceeds nature. Thank and salute them earnestly from me, and to those of your own household, please add Messrs. John and Charles Wesley, Dr. Coke, etc. That the Lord would fill you with His choicest blessings, as you have done me, is, my dear friend, the earnest prayer of your poor pensioner.

PS. Mr. Perronet wants me to fill up his letter. I would gladly do it, but at this time a sleepless night and a constant toothache unfit me for almost any thing but lying down under the cross, kissing the rod, and rejoicing in hope of a better state, in this world or in the next. But perhaps weakness and pain are the best for me in this world. The Lord will choose for me, and I fully set my heart and seal to His choice. Let us not faint in the day of adversity. The Lord tries us so that our faith may be found purged from all the dross of self-will and may work by that love which beareth all things and thinketh evil of nothing. Our calling is to follow the Crucified, and we must be crucified with Him until body and soul know the power of His resurrection, and pain and death are done away.

I hope my dear friend will make, with me, a constant choice of the following mottos of St. Paul—"Christ is gain in life and death"—"Our life is hid with Christ in God"—"If we suffer with Him, we shall also reign with Him"—"We glory in tribulation"—"God will give us rest with Christ, in that day"—"We are saved by hope." And I hope that Miss Thornton will always, by word and deed, stand to her motto, and rejoice in the Lord our God, Creator, Redeemer, and Sanctifier. To Him let us give glory *in the fires*. Amen.

To Mr. Thomas York

Nyon, July 18th, 1779

My Dear Sir—Providence is still gracious to me, and raises me friends on all sides. May God reward them all, and may you have a *double reward* for all your kindness. I hope I am getting a little strength. The Lord has blessed to me a species of black cherry, which I have eaten in large quantities... For a fortnight past I have catechized the children of the town every day, and I do not find much inconvenience from that exercise. Some of them seem to be under sweet drawings of the Father; and a few of their mothers begin to come and desire me, with tears in their eyes, to stay in this country. They urge much my being born here, but I reply that I was *born again* in England. Therefore, England is to me the dearer of the two countries.

My friends have prevailed on me to publish a Poem on the Praises of God which I wrote many years ago. The revising it for the press is at once a business and a pleasure, which I go through on horseback. Help me by your prayers to ask a blessing on this little attempt; and may the God of all grace, Who deserves so much our praises for the unspeakable Gift of His dear Son, give us such a spirit of thankful praise that we may bless and praise Him as David did formerly... I am, my dear friend, your obliged servant.

To a Nobleman

Nyon, Dec. 15th, 1779

My Lord—If the American Colonies and the West India Islands are rent from the crown, there will not grow one ear of corn the less in Great Britain. We shall still have the necessaries of life, and, what is more, the Gospel and liberty to hear it. If the great springs of trade and wealth are cut off, good men will bear that loss without much sorrow. Springs of wealth are always springs of luxury which, sooner or later, destroy the empires corrupted by wealth. Moral good may come out of our losses; I wish you may see it in England. People on the Continent imagine they see it already in English travelers, who are said to behave with more wisdom and less haughtiness than they were used to do.

Last year saw the death of three great men of these parts: Rousseau, Voltaire, and Baron Haller, a senator of Berne. The last, who is not much known in England, was a great philosopher, a profound politician, and an agreeable poet; but he was particularly famous for his skill in botany, anatomy, and physic. He has enriched the republic of letters by such a number of publications in Latin and German that the catalog of them is alone a pamphlet.

This truly great man has given another proof of the truth of Lord Bacon's assertion that, "although smatterers in philosophy are often impious, true philosophers are always religious." I have met with an old, pious, apostolic Clergyman who was intimate with the Baron and used to accompany him over the Alps, in his rambles after the wonders of nature. "With what pleasure," said the minister, "did we admire and adore the wisdom of the God of nature, and sanctify our researches by the sweet praises of the God of grace!"

When the Emperor passed this way, he stabbed Voltaire to the heart by not paying him a visit; but he waited on Haller, was two hours with him, and heard from him such pious talk as he never heard from half the philosophers of the age. The Baron was then ill of the disorder which afterwards carried him off.

Upon his deathbed, he went through sore conflicts about his interest in Christ. He sent to the old minister, requesting his most fervent prayers and wishing him to find the way through the dark valley smoother than he found it himself. However, in his last moments he expressed a renewed confidence in God's mercy through Christ, and died in peace. The old clergyman added that he thought the Baron went through this conflict to humble him thoroughly, and perhaps to chastise him for having sometimes given way to a degree of self-complacence at the thought of his amazing parts, and of the respect they procured him from the learned world. He was obliged to become last in his own eyes that he might become first and truly great in the sight of the Lord. I am, my Lord, etc.

TO MR. GREAVES

Nyon, December 25th, 1779

MY DEAR BROTHER—Glory be to God for His unspeakable Gift! May that Jesus, that eternal, all-creating, all-supporting, all-atoning, all-comforting Word, which was with God, and is God, and came in likeness of sinful flesh to dwell among men, and to be our Emmanuel, God with us; may He by a lively faith be formed in our hearts, and by a warm love lie and grow in the manger of our emptiness, filling it always with the bread that comes down from heaven!

Though absent in body I am with you and the flock in the spirit. You are now at the Lord's table. O! may all the dear souls you have just now preached to receive Jesus Christ in the pledge of His dying love, and go home with this lively conviction: "God has given me eternal life, and this life is in His Son. He that hath the Son hath life: I have the Son, I have life, even eternal life. The way, the truth, the life, and happiness are mine. And now, return unto thy rest, O my soul. Lord, let thy servant depart in peace; for mine eyes—the eyes of my faith have seen, the hand of my faith hath handled, the mouth of my faith hath tasted Thy salvation—a salvation present, unspeakable, and eternal."

Glory be to God in Heaven! Peace on earth! Love and goodwill everywhere, but especially in the spot where Providence has called us to cry, "Behold, what manner of love the Father has testified to us, in Jesus, that we, children of wrath, should be made children of God, by that only begotten Son of the Most High, Who was born for our regeneration, crucified for our atonement, raised for our justification, and now triumphs in Heaven for our full redemption and for our eternal glorification." To Him be glory for ever and ever; and may all who fear and love Him about you say for ever, "Amen! Hallelujah!"

Out of the fullness of my heart I invite them to do so, but how shallow is my fullness to His! What a drop to an ocean without bottom or shore! Let us, then, receive continually from

Him Who is the overflowing and ever present source of pardoning, sanctifying, and exhilarating grace. From the foot of the Wrekin where you are, to the foot of the Alps where I am, let us echo back to each other the joyful, thankful cry of the primitive Christians (which was the text here this morning), "Out of His fullness we have all received grace for grace."

I long to hear from you and the flock. How do you go on? Answer this and my last together, and let me know that you cast joyfully your burdens on the Lord...

Our Lord Lieutenant, being stirred up by some of the clergy, and believing firmly that I am banished from England, has taken the alarm still more, and forbidden the ministers to let me exhort in their houses, threatening them with the power of the senate if they did. They all yielded, but are now ashamed of it. A young clergyman, a true Timothy, has opened me his house, where I exhort twice a week; and the other clergymen, encouraged by his boldness, come to our meetings.

Give my kind pastoral love to all my people in general, and particularly to all who fear God and love Jesus and the brethren. May all see, and see more abundantly, the salvation of God. May national distress be sanctified to them; and may they all be loyal subjects of the King of kings, and of His anointed—our King. May the approaching New Year be to them a year of peace and Gospel grace... That you and the flock may fare well in Jesus is the hearty prayer of yours.

To Mr. Greaves

Nyon, March 7th, 1780

My Dear Brother—I long to hear from you. I hope you are well and grow in the love of Christ and of the souls bought with His blood which are committed to your care. May you have the comfort of bringing them all into the pastures of the Gospel and seeing them thrive under your pastoral care. I recommend to your care the most helpless of the flock—I mean the children and the sick. They most need your help, and they are the most likely to benefit by it; for affliction softens the heart, and children are not yet quite hardened through the deceitfulness of sin.

I beg you will not fail, when you have opportunity, to recommend to our flock that they honor the King, study to be quiet, and hold up, as much as lies in them, the hands of the government by which we are protected. Remember me kindly to Mr. Gilpin, and to all our parishioners. God give you peace by all means as, in His mercy, He does to your affectionate friend and fellow-laborer.

To Mr. Greaves

Nyon, Sept. 15th, 1780

My Dear Fellow-Laborer—I had fixed the time of my departure for this month, but now two hindrances stand in my way. When I came to collect the parts of my manuscript, I found the most considerable part wanting. And so, after a thousand searches, I was obliged to write it over again. This accident obliged me to put off my journey, and now the change of weather has brought back some symptoms of my disorder…

Have patience then a little while. If things are not as you could wish, you can do as I have done for many years—*learn patience by the things which you suffer.* Crossing our will, getting the better of our own inclinations, and growing in experience are no mean advantages, and they may all be yours. Mr. Ireland writes me word that if I return to England now, the winter will undo all I have been doing for my health for many years. However, I have not quite laid aside the design of spending the winter at Madeley. I am firmly purposed that if I do not set out this autumn, I will do so, God willing, next spring as early as I can.

Till I had this relapse, I was able, thank God, to exhort in a private room three times a week. However, the Lord Lieutenant will not allow me to get into a pulpit, though they permit the schoolmasters, who are laymen, to put on a band and read the church prayers—so high runs the prejudice. The clergy tell me that if I will renounce my ordination and get Presbyterian orders among them they will allow me to preach. On these terms one of the ministers of this town offers me his curacy. A young clergyman of Geneva, tutor to my nephew, appears to me a truly converted man. He is so pleased when I tell him there are converted souls in England, that he will go over with me to learn English and converse with the British Christians. He wrote last summer with such force to some of the clergy who were stirring up the fire of persecution, that he made them ashamed, and we have since had peace from that quarter.

There is little genuine piety in these parts. Nevertheless, there is yet some of the form of it in that they go to the Lord's table regularly four times a year. There meet the adulterers, the drunkards, the swearers, the infidels, and even the materialists. They have no idea of the double damnation that awaits hypocrites. They look upon partaking that sacrament as a ceremony enjoined by the magistrate.

At Zürich, the first town of this country, they have lately beheaded a clergyman who wanted to betray his country to the emperor to whom it chiefly belonged. It is the town of the great reformer Zwingli; yet there they poisoned the sacramental wine a few years ago. Tell it not in Gath! I mention this to show you that there is occasion and great need to bear a testimony against the faults of the clergy here; and if I cannot do it from the pulpit, I must try to do it from the press. Their canons, which were composed by two hundred and thirty pastors at the time of the reformation, are so spiritual and apostolic that I design to translate them into English, if I am spared.

Farewell, my dear brother. Take care, good, constant care, of the flock committed to your charge, especially the *sick* and the *young*. Salute all our dear parishioners. Let me still have a part in your prayers—public and private. Rejoice in the Lord as, through grace, I am enabled to do in all my little tribulations. I am your affectionate friend and fellow-laborer.

TO THE SOCIETIES IN AND ABOUT MADELEY

Nyon, Sept. 15, 1780

MY DEAR BRETHREN—Grace and peace, truth and love be multiplied unto you all. Stand fast in the Lord my dear brethren. Stand fast to Jesus. Stand fast to one another. Stand fast to the vow we have so often renewed together upon our knees and at the Lord's table. Resolve to save yourselves *altogether*. Don't be *so unloving, so cowardly*, as to let one of your little company fall into the hands of the world and the devil. Agree to crucify the body of sin together.

I am still in a strait between the work which Providence cuts out for me here and the love which draws me to you. When I shall have the pleasure of seeing you, let it not be embittered by the sorrow of finding any of you half-hearted and lukewarm. Let me find you all strong in the Lord and increased in humble love. Salute from me all that followed with us fifteen years ago. Care still for your old brethren. Let there be no Cain among you, no Esau, no Lot's wife. Let the love of David and Jonathan, heightened by that of Martha, Mary, Lazarus, and our Lord, shine in all your thoughts, your tempers, your words, your looks, and your actions. If you love one another, your little meetings will be a renewed feast; and the God of love, Who is peculiarly present where two or three are gathered together in the name of Jesus and in the spirit of love, will abundantly bless you. Bear me still upon your breasts in prayer, as I do you upon mine; and rejoice with me that the Lord Who made, redeemed, and comforts us, *bears us all upon His*. I am yours in Him.

TO MR. JOHN OWEN

Nyon, Feb. 14th, 1781

DEAR BROTHER—I thank you for your kind lines. I have deferred answering them till I could inform you of the time of my departure hence, which you will see in my letter to Mr. Wase. I hope you help both Mr. Greaves and the preachers to stir up the people in my parish. Be *much* in prayer. Strengthen the things that remain and are ready to die. I hope you take counsel with Michael Onions, Mrs. Palmer, and Molly Cartwright about the most effectual means to recover the backsliders and to keep together to Christ and to each other those who still hold their shield. Salute them kindly from me, and tell them that I hope they will give me a good account of their little companies and of themselves.

If I were not a minister, I would be a *schoolmaster*, to have the pleasure of bringing up children in the fear of the Lord. That pleasure is yours. Relish it, and it will comfort and strengthen you in your work. The joy of the Lord and of charity is our strength. Salute the children from me, and tell them that I long to show them the way to happiness and Heaven.

Pray have you mastered the stiffness and shyness of your temper? Charity gives a meekness, an affability, a childlike simplicity and openness which nature has denied you, that grace might have all the honor of it. Let me find you shining by these virtues, and you will revive me much. God bless your labor about the sheep and the lambs… Remember me to all friends. I am yours affectionately.

To the Brethren at Madeley Church

Nyon, Feb. 14th, 1781

My Dear Brethren—My heart leaps for joy at the thought of coming to see you and bless the Lord with you. Let us not stay to praise Him till we see each other. Let us see Him in His Son, in His Word, in His works, and in all the members of Christ. How slow will post-horses go in comparison of love!

> Quick as seraphic flames we move,
> To reign with Christ in endless day.

Meet me, as I do you—in spirit; and we shall not stay till April or May to bless God together. Now will be the time of union and love.

To Mr. William Wase

Nyon, Feb. 14th, 1781

My Dear Friend—I thank you for your kind remembrance of me. I need not be urged to return; brotherly love draws me to Madeley, and circumstances drive me hence. With pleasure I see the days lengthen, and hasten the happy hour when I shall see the little flock rejoicing in God as, through mercy, I do. I am exceeding glad that there is a revival on your side the water, and that you are obliged to enlarge your room.

I wish I could contribute to shake the dry bones in my parish, but I have no confidence in the flesh. What I could not do when I was in my strength I have little prospect of doing now that my strength is broken. However, I don't despair, for the work is not *mine* but *the Lord's*. If the few who love the Gospel would be simple and zealous, God would again hear their prayers for those who are content to go on in the broad way. I thank you for your view of the iron bridge. I hope the word and the faith that works by love will erect a more solid and durable bridge to unite those who travel together towards Zion.

My friend Ireland invites me to go and join him in the South of France, and I long to see whether I could not have more liberty to preach the word among the Papists than among the Protestants. But it is so little I can do, that I doubt much whether it is worth while going so far upon so little a chance. If I were stronger and had more time, the fear of *being hanged* should not detain me...

O! my friend, give yourself wholly up to the Lord, and you will have that peace and joy, through Christ and righteousness, which will be worth a little heaven to you. Adieu.

To Mr. Michael Onions

Nyon, March, 1781

My Dear Brother—I thank you for your kind remembrance of me, and for your letters. I hope to bring my fuller thanks to you in person. Come, hold up your hands. Confirm the feeble knees. Set up an Ebenezer every hour of the day. In everything give thanks. In order to this, pray without ceasing and rejoice evermore.

My heart sympathizes with poor Molly Cartwright. Tell her from me that her husband lives in Him Who is the resurrection, and that I want her to live *there*, with him. In Christ there is no death, but the victory over death. O! let us live in Him, to Him, for Him, Who more than repairs all our losses. I long to rejoice with her in hopes of meeting our departed friends, where parting and trouble shall be no more.

My love to your wife. Tell her she promised me to be Jesus's as well as yours. I trust her mother ripens faster for glory than for the grave. I hope to find her quite mellowed by the humble love of the Gospel. My love to John Owen and all our other leaders, and by them to the few who do not tire by the way. With regard to the others, take them in the arms of prayer and love, and carry them out of Egypt and Sodom if they are loath to come. Despair of none. You know charity hopeth all things, and brings many things to pass. All things are *possible* to him that believeth, all things are *easy* to him that loveth. God be with you, my dear brother, and make you faithful unto death. It is my prayer for you, and all the society, and all my dear neighbors, my dear parishioners, to whom I beg to be remembered. I have no place to write their names, but I pray they may be all written in the book of life. God is merciful, gracious, and faithful. I set my seal to His loving kindness. Witness my heart and hand.

TO WILLIAM PERRONET

Lyons, April 6th, 1781

MY DEAR FRIEND—We are both weak and afflicted, but Jesus careth for us. He is every where, and here He has all power to deliver us, and He may do it by ways we little think of. "As Thou wilt, when Thou wilt, and where Thou wilt," said Baxter. Let us say the same. It was of the Lord you did not come with me, for you would have been sick as I am. I am overdone with riding and preaching. I preached twice in the fields. I carry home with me much weakness and a pain in my back, which I fear will end in the grave. The Lord's will be done. I know I am called to suffer and die. The journey tires me, but through mercy I bear it. Let us believe and rejoice in the Lord Jesus.

TO A FRIEND

Madeley, June 12th, 1781

MY VERY DEAR FRIEND—I stayed longer at Brislington than I designed. Mr. Ireland was ill, but would nevertheless come with me, so that I was obliged to stay till he was better. Indeed it was well I did not come without him; for he has helped me to regulate my outward affairs, which were in great confusion. Mr. Greaves leaves me. I will either leave Madeley or have an assistant able to stir among the people, for I had much rather be gone than stay here to see the dead bury their dead. Well, we shall soon remove out of all and rest from our little cares and labors.

You do not forget, I hope, that you have need of patience, as well as I, to inherit the promises, the best and greatest of which are not sealed but to such as keep the word of Christ's patience and such as persevere with Him in His temptations. Hold on then, patient faith and joyful hope! If I were by you, I would preach to your heart and my own a lecture on this text, "We are saved by hope," and by a faith which is never stronger than when it is contrary to all the feelings of flesh and blood.

Pray what news of the glory? Does the glory of the Lord fill the temple, your house, your heart? A cloud is over my poor parish; but alas! it is not the luminous cloud by day, nor the pillar of fire by night. Even the few remaining professors stared at me the other day when I preached to them on these words, "Ye shall receive the Holy Ghost, for the promise is unto you." Well, the promise is unto us; if others despise it, still let us believe and hope. Nothing enlarges the heart and awakens the soul more than that believing, loving expectation. Let us wait together until we are all endued with power from on high.

To Mr. Rankin

Madeley, June 25th, 1781

My Dear Brother—I thank you for your kind remembrance of me and for your letter to me. I found myself of one heart with you, both as a preacher and believer, before I left Bristol; and I am glad you find freedom to speak to me as your friend in Christ. By what you mention of your experience, I am confirmed in the thought that 1. It is often harder to keep in the way of faith and light than to get into it. 2. That speculation and reasoning hinder us to get into that way, and lead us out of it when we are in it. 3. The only business of those who come to God, as a Redeemer or Sanctifier, must be to feel their want of redemption and sanctifying power from on high, and to come for it by simple, cordial, working faith.

Easily the heart gets into a false rest before our last enemy is overcome. Hence arises a relapsing, in an imperceptible degree, into indolence and carnal security. Hence a dreaming that we are rich and increased in goods. This is one of the causes of declension you perceive among some of the Methodists. Another is the outward rest they have, which is consistent with the selfish views of hypocrites and with the unbending of the bow of faith in those who are sincere. Another may be the judging of the greatness of the work by the numbers in society. Be the consequence what it will, those who see the evil should honestly bear their testimony against it, first in their own souls, next by their life, and thirdly by their plain and constant reproofs and exhortations.

The work of justification seems stopped, in some degree, because the glory and necessity of the pardon of sins, to be received and enjoyed now by faith, is not pressed enough upon sinners, and the need of retaining it upon believers. The work of sanctification is hindered, if I am not mistaken, by the same reason. It is hindered by holding out the being delivered from sin as the mark to be aimed at, instead of the being rooted in Christ, and the being filled with the fullness of God—with power from on high. The dispensation of the Spirit is confounded with that of the Son. Because the former is not being held forth clearly enough, formal and lukewarm believers in Jesus Christ suppose they have the gift of the Holy Ghost. Hence the increase of carnal professors (see Acts 8:16), and hence so few spiritual men. Let us pray, hope, love, believe for ourselves, and call, as you say, for the display of the Lord's arm. My love to your dear fellow-laborer, Mr. Pawson. Pray for your affectionate brother.

To Joseph Benson

Madeley, June, 1781

My Dear Brother—I rejoice and am much obliged to you for your kind remembrance of me... Happy are you if you live by faith in the atoning blood for justification and sanctification. It is the Spirit alone which can show us the worth and make us feel the powerful influence of the Savior's blood and righteousness. And, so far as my little experience goes, He gives that blessed privilege only to those who in the depth of poverty wait for that divine revelation. I learn not to despise the least beam of truth, and I quietly and joyfully wait for the bright sunshine.

The best way to avoid errors is to lie very low before God; to know His voice and consult Him in all things; learning to mortify our wise pride, as well as our aspiring will and our disordered passions. But more of this if we live to see each other again...

A godly wife is a peculiar blessing from the Lord. I wish you joy for such a loan. Possess it with godly fear and holy joy; and the God that gave her you help you both to see your doubled piety take root in the heart of the child that crowns your union. So prays, my dear brother, your affectionate friend.

To Miss Perronet

Madeley, Sept. 4th, 1781

My Dear Friend—You want "some *thoughts* on the love of God," and I want the warmest *feelings* of it. Let us believe His creating, feel His preserving, admire His redeeming, and triumph in His sanctifying love. Loving is the best way to grow in love. Look we, then, at the love of our heavenly Father, shining in the face of our elder Brother, and we shall be changed into love, His image and nature, from one *glorious* and *glorifying* degree of love to another. Love always delights in the object loved. "Delight thou in the Lord," then, "and thou shall have thy heart's desire;" for we can desire nothing more than the *supreme good* and *infinite bliss*. Both are in God. When, therefore, we love God truly, we delight in what He is, we share in His infinite happiness. And by divine sympathy His throne of glory becomes ours; for true love rejoices in all the joy of the object it cleaves to.

Add to this, that, when we love God, we have always our hearts desire; for we love His will, His desires become ours, and ours are always perfectly resigned to His. Now as God does whatever He pleases both in Heaven and earth, His lovers have always their hearts desire, forasmuch as they always have His will, which is theirs. Submitting our private will to His is only preferring a greater good to a less, as our Lord did in the garden; and we are all called to do it in afflictions. Farewell, my dear friend, and excuse these reflections, which you could make much better than your humble servant.

TO LADY MARY FITZGERALD

Madeley, Sept. 29th, 1781

MY DEAR AND HONORED FRIEND—You have been in the fire of affliction, where faith is tried, where patient hope is exercised, and where perfect love, which casts out fear, and endureth all things, is proved worthy of Him Who made bare His breast and said to His Father, "Lo! I come to do Thy will, O God!" I come to be obedient unto death, even the painful, shameful death of the cross.

Continue to offer your body as a living, or if it please God, as a lingering, dying sacrifice to Him Who has decreed that if we will reign with Christ, we must suffer with Him. This is our reasonable service; for it would be absurd that our Lord should have been perfected by sufferings, thorns, and the cross, and that we should have nothing but enjoyment, roses, and a crown. How faithful, how merciful is our God! He brings you once more from the verge of eternity: well, my dear friend, I welcome you back into life, and into the enjoyment of farther opportunities of receiving and doing good—of growing in grace, and perfecting holiness in the fear of the Lord.

Chastened, spared like you, and more and more convinced that I am helplessness itself, and that there is help laid on our Surety and Savior for us, I invite you to say with me—"When I am weak, Christ my life is strong still; for me to live shall be Christ, and to die gain." Dear Madam, to know the bare cross is uncomfortable. But to know and gather the fruit of that tree is life from the dead, it is more abundant life after fainting. Let us then know, i.e. consider, and embrace Jesus Christ crucified to make an end of sin—shedding tears and His most precious blood to cleanse us from all sin; to trace again the divine image, goodness, love, and happiness on our souls, and to seal our firm title to glory.

"Not a text," say you, "came to me, only I knew none perished at His feet." Then you remembered Christ, the sum and substance of all the Scriptures. Then you believed on Him in Whom all the sweetest texts and all the promises are yea and amen. O believe more steadily, more confidently. Dare even to obey the apostolic precept, "Reckon yourselves dead indeed unto sin, but alive to God by Jesus Christ our Lord." Embrace with more earnestness the righteousness of faith, and you will have more peace and joy in the Holy Ghost. Rejoice in Christ your peace. Yea, rejoice in God your Savior. And if there is a needs be for your being in heaviness for a season, rejoice in tribulation—"sorrowful but always rejoicing." "When I am destitute of all comfort, this shall yield me comfort," said Kempis, "that Thy will is done." If Abraham believed in hope against hope—that is against human, natural hope—can you not, through grace, as a daughter of Abraham, rejoice in heavenly hope against all natural feelings, and even against all temptations? "Count it all joy," says St. James, "when you fall into divers temptations and trials." Don't be afraid of the storm. Christ is in the ship; and He does not sleep, as unbelief is apt to fancy.

I thank you, my dear Lady, for your friendly wish of leaving your clay here. I return it by wishing you may leave all the body of sin now in that mysterious grotto of mount Calvary, where myriads of sinners have buried their doubts, their fears, and their old man. Prop up your clay a little longer; for I want to sing with you, "Salvation to God and the Lamb." I want you to help me, with the understanding and the voice, to witness that Jesus "saves to the uttermost all who come to God through Him;" that He cannot only make an end of sin, but bring in an everlasting, triumphant righteousness… I am, my dear lady, your obedient, affectionate servant.

To Lady Mary Fitzgerald

Madeley, Sept. 31st, 1781

My Much Honored Lady—Yesterday I received the honor of your letter without date, which has been, I am told, waiting here some time. What a pity I did not rejoice sooner in the good news you send me, that you desire to be *entirely* devoted to God. Indeed, complaints follow; but *Heaven* is in that holy desire. If you cultivate it, it will produce all that conformity to a holy God which love can bring to a human soul, called to partake the divine nature. As for your complaints, they are the natural expressions of that repentance which precedes in our hearts the coming of the Comforter, Who is to abide with us for ever. I am ready to rejoice, or to mourn with my honored friend. I have abundant cause to do both with respect to myself, my ministrations, the Church, and my people.

And will you, indeed, find it in your heart to honor my house with your presence, and perfume also with your prayers the plain apartments occupied by your friend Johnson? I wonder at nothing on earth when I consider the condescension with which Emmanuel came down from Heaven and filled a stable with His glory. Your time, my condescending friend, will suit me best. You will be queen in my hermitage, the Lord will rule in our hearts, and you will command under Him within our walls.

You smile, perhaps, at the vastness of your new empire. But if you can be content and happy in God in my homely solitude, you will make greater advances towards bliss than if you obtained the principality of Wales. But if you cannot be happy with Jesus, prayer, praise, godly conversation, and retirement, expect a disappointment. However, my honored friend, if you come, come as the serious Catholics go on a pilgrimage, as French noblemen go to the Carthusian convent at La Trappe, as the French king's aunts went to the Carmelites. Come and do *evangelical penance*. Our good friend Johnson will tell you of an upper room where we crucify our old man and have had many a visit from the new. If you do not bring her with you, bring her faith, which brought him down, and then you shall not pine for the company of earthly princes. The Prince of peace and life Himself will keep His court in our cottage, and your heart shall be one of His favorite thrones.

To Mr. Vincent Perronet

Madeley, Dec., 1781

Rev. and Dear Sir—While I condole with you about the death of my dear friend, your dear son, I congratulate you about the resignation and Christian fortitude with which you, Abraham-like, lay him upon the altar of our heavenly Father's providential, good, and acceptable will. We shall one day see why He made your sons go before you, and my kind physician before me. About the time he died, so far as I can find by your kind letter, a strong concern about him fell upon me by day and by night, insomuch that I could not help waking my wife to join me in praying for him; and at once that concern ceased, nor have I since had any such spiritual feeling. I therefore concluded that the conflict I supposed my friend to be in was ended. But how surprised was I to find it was by death! Well! whether Paul or Apollos, whether life or death, all things are ours through Jesus. He knows how to bring good out of evil, and how to blow us into the harbor by a cross wind and even by a dreadful storm.

If, my dear friend, your son has not quite completed his affairs in Switzerland and an agent is necessary there for that purpose, I offer you the care and help of my brother, who was our counselor. I am sure he will do what lies in him to oblige the father of him whom he had the pleasure of having some time under his roof as a sick monument of Christian meekness and resignation.

I am but poorly, though I serve yet my Church without a curate, Mr. Bailey being needed at Kingswood. But what are we? Poor mortals, dying in the midst of a world of dying and dead men. But in the midst of death we are in Christ the "resurrection and the life," to Whom be glory for ever. So prays, Rev. and dear sir, your affectionate son and servant in the Gospel.

To the Hon. Mrs. C——

Cross Hall, Yorkshire, Dec. 26th, 1781

My Very Dear Friend—Your favor of the 4th instant did not reach me until a considerable time after date, through my being still absent from Madeley. A clergyman of this neighborhood made an exchange with me to facilitate my settling some affairs of a temporal nature in this country. The kind part you take in my happiness demands my warmest thanks; and I beg you will accept them multiplied by those which my dear Partner presents to you. Yes, my dear friend, I am married in my old age, and have a new opportunity of considering a great mystery in the most perfect type of our Lord's mystical union with His Church. I have now a new call to pray for a fullness of Christ's holy, gentle, meek, loving Spirit, that I may love my wife as He loved His Spouse, the Church.

But the emblem is greatly deficient. The Lamb is worthy of His spouse, and more than worthy; whereas I must acknowledge myself unworthy of the yoke-fellow whom Heaven has reserved for me. She is a person after my own heart; and I make no doubt we shall increase the number of the happy marriages in the Church Militant. Indeed they are not so many, but it may be worth a Christian's while to add one more to the number. God declared it was not good that man, a social being, should live alone, and therefore He gave him a help meet for him. For the same reason our Lord sent forth His disciples two and two. Had I searched the three kingdoms, I could not have found one brother willing to share gratis my weal, woe, and labors, and complaisant enough to unite his fortunes to mine. But God has found me a partner, "a sister, a wife," to use St. Paul's language, who is not afraid to face with me the colliers and bargemen of my parish until death part us.

Buried together in our country village, we shall help one another to trim our lamps and wait, as I trust you do continually, for the coming of the heavenly Bridegroom. Well, for us the heavenly Child is born, to us a double Son is given, and with Him the double Kingdom of grace and glory. O my dear friends, let us press into and meet in both of these kingdoms. Our Surety and Savior is the way and the door into them; and blessed be free grace, the way is free, as the King's highway, and the door open, like the arms of Jesus crucified.

January 1st, 1782. I live, blessed be God, to devote myself again to His blessed service in this world, or in the next, and to wish my dear friends all the blessings of a year of Jubilee. Whatever this year bring forth, may it bring us the fullest measures of salvation attainable on earth, and the most complete preparation for Heaven. I have a solemn call to gird my loins and keep my lamp burning. Strangely restored to health and strength considering my years; by the good nursing of my dear Partner, I ventured to preach of late as often as I did formerly. After having read prayers and preached twice on Christmas day, etc., I did last Sunday what I had never done—I continued doing duty from 10:00 till past 4:00 in the afternoon, owing to christenings, churchings, and the sacrament, which I administered to a church full of people. So that I was obliged to go from the communion table to begin the evening service, and then to visit some sick.

This has brought back upon me one of my old, dangerous symptoms, so that I had flattered myself in vain to do the whole duty of my own parish. My dear wife is nursing me with the tenderest care, gives me up to God with the greatest resignation, and helps me to rejoice that life and death, health and sickness, work all for our good. They are all "ours" as blessed instruments to forward us in our journey to Heaven.

We intend to set out for Madeley tomorrow. The prospect of a winter's journey is not sweet, but the prospect of meeting you and your dear sister… and our other companions in tribulation in Heaven is delightful. The Lord prepare and fit us for that glorious meeting! … Believe me to be, my dear Friend and Fellow traveler to Zion, your most obliged and affectionate servant.

TO LADY MARY FITZGERALD

Madeley, Jan., 1782

MY HONORED FRIEND—I thank you for your kind congratulations on my marriage. The Lord has indeed blessed me with a Partner after my own heart—dead to the world, and wanting, as well as myself, to be filled with all the life of God. She joins me in dutiful thanks to your Ladyship for your obliging remembrance of her in your kind letter, and will help me to welcome you to the little hermitage we spoke of last year in London, if your Ladyship's health or taste should call you to retire for a while from the hurry of the town.

What a difference between the court of the King of kings and that of King George! How peaceable the former; how full of hurry the latter! The Prince Himself welcomes us and manifests Himself to us as Prince of Peace, as Emmanuel, God with us. He will even bring His Kingdom and keep His court in our hearts. If we open them by the attention and recollection of faith, He will even sup with us and make us taste the sweetness of that bread which came down from Heaven, and the virtue of the blood which cleanses from all sin. That this may be our constant experience, and that of our dear companions in tribulation in St. James's Place, is the sincere and frequent wish of, my Lady, your most obliged and obedient servant.

TO LADY MARY FITZGERALD

Madeley, Aug. 28th, 1782

MY HONORED FRIEND—Grace, mercy, and humble love be multiplied to you from God our Father, and from our Lord Jesus Christ, through the eternal Spirit, in whose name we were baptized into the body of the Church, the Spouse of the Son of God. The Lord has peculiar favors in store for your Ladyship and for me. The proof is that we are *afflicted*. Have you been in a weak state of health? I have had the honor to drink of your cup. The influenza has laid me down, but the Lord has raised me up again. And when I was partly well, I broke my shin accidentally (should I not say providentially) against a bench, and the consequence was my being confined by a bad leg to my bed, whence I write these lines. O may they be lines of consolation to my dear friend! May the God of all Grace, Who comforts unworthy me, rejoice your oppressed heart and make it overflow with His patient love and sanctifying truth.

You still complain of *vile self.* I wish you joy for your knowing your enemy. Let vile self be reduced to *order*, and though he be a bad master, he will become an *excellent servant.* If you say, "How shall I do this?" I reply, by letting the Lord, the Maker, the Preserver, the Redeemer, the Lover of your soul, ascend upon the throne of your thoughts, will, and affections. Who deserves to engross and fill them better than He does? Is He not your first Lord, your best Husband, your most faithful Friend, and your greatest Benefactor? If you say, "I do not see Him;" I reply that you never saw the soul of any of your friends—nor do you see even the body of him whom you call your idol. O! allow Jehovah, the Supreme Being, to be to you what He deserves to be, *all in all.* One lively act of faith; one assent and consent to this delightful truth, that your Father Who is in Heaven loves you a thousand times more than you love your idol (for God's love is like Himself—*infinite and boundless*), will set your heart at liberty and even make it dance for joy.

What if, to this ravishing consideration, you add the transporting truth that the Son of God, fairer than the sons of men and brighter than angels, has loved you unto death—to the death of the cross, and loves you still, more than all your friends do, were their love collected into one heart: could you help thinking, with a degree of joyous gratitude, of such an instance of divine condescension? No, your vile self would be ennobled, raised, expanded, and set at liberty by this evangelical thought, and if you did not destroy this divine conception, if you nourished this little degree of the love of Christ, Emmanuel, the God of love, would be more fully manifested in you, and salvation would from this moment grow in your soul. Jesus would grow in your believing, loving heart. Self would be nobody; Emmanuel would be all in all. Then Lady Mary would share all the happiness and, e'er long, all the glory of that favored virgin whom all the nations shall call blessed. You bear her name; let her Son, by the incorruptible seed of the word, be also formed in you through faith; and you will be so taken up by this wonder of divine love, so employed in praising your Father's mercy, and Savior's love and tenderness, that you will have but little time to speak either of *good or bad self*. When self is forgotten as nothing before God, you put self in its proper place; and you make room for the heavenly Being whose holy and happy existence you are to shadow out.

If you have left off attending on the Princess, attend on the Prince of peace with double diligence. If you have been wanting in that sweet and honorable duty, it is because the enemy has told you lies of your Savior, and has cast a veil over the love of His heart and the beauty of His face. See the snare and avoid it…

To Rev. Charles Wesley

Madeley, Dec. 19th, 1782

Rev. and Dear Sir—I thank you for your hint about exemplifying the love of Christ and His Church. I hope we do. I was afraid, at first, to say much of the matter, for new married people do not at first know each other. But having now lived fourteen months in my new state, I can tell you that Providence has reserved a *prize* for me, and that my wife is far better to me than the Church to Christ. So that if the parallel fails it will be on my side.

Be so good as to peruse the enclosed sheets. Mr. De Luc, to whom they are addressed, is Reader to the Queen and the author of some volumes of Letters to her. He is a true philosopher. I flatter myself that he will present my letter to the Queen. Do you find anything *improper* in the addition I have made to my poem? I wish I were near you for your criticisms. You would direct me, both as a poet and a Frenchman.

I have yet strength enough to do my parish duty without the help of a Curate. O that the Lord would help me to do it acceptably and profitably! The colliers begun to rise in this neighborhood. Happily the cockatrice's egg was crushed before the serpent came out. However, I got many a hearty curse from the colliers for the plain words I spoke on that occasion. I want to see days of power both *within* and *without*. But in the mean time I would follow closely my light in the narrow path. My wife joins me in respectful love to Mrs. Wesley and yourself, and requesting an interest in your prayers for us I remain, my dear Sir, your affectionate, obliged brother, servant, and son in the Gospel.

To Mrs. Thornton

Madeley, March 3rd, 1783

My Dear Friend—Yesterday I received your melancholy yet joyful letter as I came from the sacrament, where the grace of God had armed me to meet the awful news. And is my merciful host gone to reap the fruit of his mercy to me? I thought I should have been permitted to go first and welcome him into everlasting habitations. But Providence has ordered it otherwise, and I am left behind to say, with you and dear Mrs. Greenwood, "The Lord gave, and has taken away, and blessed be His holy Name!"

The glory with which his setting sun was gilded is the greatest comfort by which Heaven could alleviate his loss. Let me die as he did, and let my last end be like his! I was so sensibly affected by your account that I could not help reading part of your letter at church in the afternoon, and desiring all the congregation to join me in thanksgiving for the late mercies he had vouchsafed to my generous benefactor. On such occasions let sighs be lost in praise, and repining in humble submission and thankful acquiescence. I hope dear Mrs. Greenwood mixes a tear of joy with a tear of sorrow. Who would not be landed on the other side the stream of time, if he were sure of such a passage? Who would wish his best friend back on the shores of sorrow so triumphantly left by Mr. Greenwood?

I hope Mr. Thomas Greenwood and his brother Josiah have been rooted and grounded in their good purposes by their dying father's exhortations and charges. Pray give my kindest love to them both, and tell them that I join my entreaties to his that they would take to and keep in the way that brought their parent peace and joy at the last.

So Mr. and Mrs. Perronet are no more, and Lazarus is still alive! What scenes does this world afford? But the most amazing is certainly that of Emmanuel crucified, and offering *us* pardons and crowns of glory. May we ever gaze at that wonderful object until it has formed us into love, peace, and joy! We thank you for the sweet name you still call us by, and we heartily take the hint and subscribe ourselves your affectionate, grateful friends and ready servants in Christ.

TO LADY MARY FITZGERALD

Dublin, Aug. 23rd, 1783

HONORED AND DEAR MADAM—I see the truth of those words of our Lord, "In me ye shall have peace," comfort, strength, and joy. "Be of good cheer." We came here to see the members of our Lord, and we find you removed—and removing farther still than you now are. What does this providence teach us? I learn that I must rejoice in the Lord above all His members, and find them all in Him Who fills all in all. He is the life of all our friends, the joy of all our brethren. If our Lord is your life, your strength, and your all, you will remove in vain to the North or South. You cannot go from your spiritual friends; they will meet you in the common center of all life and righteousness. There they will bless you, rejoice in your joy, and sympathize in your sorrow.

If Providence calls you to England by Scotland, by which route your Ladyship apprehends so much difficulty, you know we must at least go to Heaven by a way equally painful—the narrow way, the way marked with blood, and with the tears and cross of the Son of God. And if we follow Him weeping, we shall return with everlasting joy on our heads. Even now the foretaste of those joys is given to us through hope, for by hope we are saved. Let our faith and hope be in God, rooted and grounded in Him Who gives vital heat to our hearts, and Who fans there the spark of grace which His mercy has kindled. And may that spark, by the inspiration of the Holy Ghost, become a fire of holy love, heavenly zeal, and heavenly glory. Such power belongeth to the Almighty. He that spared not His own Son, and has promised us His Holy Spirit, which is the mighty stream of His grace and the mighty flame of His love, will not deny us that power if we wait for it in His appointed ways and ask it in the all prevailing name of Emmanuel, God with us.

My dear partner, who, like myself, is deeply sensible of your Ladyship's kindness in remembering us, joins me in thanks for your obliging note, and in cordial wishes that all the desires of your believing soul may be granted you, both for time, death, and eternity. We subscribe ourselves with grateful sincerity, honored Madam, your devoted servants in our bleeding Lord.

To the Society in Dublin

Madeley, Nov., 1783

To all the dear Brethren who, after kindly inviting John and Mary Fletcher, patiently bearing with them and their infirmities, and entertaining them in the most hospitable, Christian manner, have added to all their former favors that of thanking them for their most pleasant and profitable journey.

Brethren and Dearly Beloved in the Lord—We had felt shame enough under the sense of your kindness and patience towards us, and of our unprofitableness towards you when at Dublin. You needed not to have added to our shame by the new token of your love—the friendly letter we have received from you. We, we are indebted to you, dear brethren. We owed you the letter of thanks which you have gratuitously sent. But in all things you will have the pre-eminence, and we are glad to drink the cup of humility at your feet. May the Lord, Who can part a sea by the touch of a rod, and could at first cause the earth to bring forth abundantly all manner of trees and plants without seed, so bless the seed of the Word which we sowed in great weakness among you as to make it produce a full crop of humble repentance, cheerful faith, triumphant hope, and the sanctifying influences of God's Spirit in your hearts, in all your families, in all your assemblies, and in your whole society! If your profuse liberality towards us abounded to the comfort of our poor brethren, we doubly rejoice on your account and on theirs.

When we see so many of your dear names, we rejoice in hopes that as they fill and confirm an epistle dictated by overflowing love, so they are enrolled on the list of the dear people whom our great High Priest bears, not on the breastplate, as Aaron, but on His bleeding hands and in His very heart, which is the overflowing and everflowing fountain of divine and brotherly love. We cannot remember your faces; we remember what will last longer than your features—your work and labor, your repasts of love, together with your prayers and sighs. May that seed sown be watered by the Redeemer's blood! We ask it with tears of gratitude and joy while we, on our bended knees, spread your names, as you have kindly put them, and your wants, so far as we remember them, before the Father of mercies and the Author of every perfect gift. Let our worthless names still find a place in your memory when you remember your brethren distant in the flesh but near in the Spirit. Among such vouchsafe to reckon, dear brethren, your very affectionate and truly obliged servants in Christ.

TO MRS. DOLIER

Madeley, Nov., 1783

DEAR FRIEND—And were my dear Brother and Sister Dolier pleased by the receipt of a letter from such an unworthy worm?

O that I could convey some word from the mouth of my adorable Lord to your hearts! O that He would permit me, His poor creature, to drop a sentence which might prove an encouragement to my dear friends in their way! You ask, "Shall I hope to attain the clean heart, and walk in purity while here below?" Why not? Abraham hoped against hope, and there sprang from him, as good as dead, as the stars of heaven for multitude. Does unbelief say, "Thou art dead; thou hast outstayed thy day, and it is all over?" Then arise out of the dust, rouse up all your powers; against hope, believe in hope, and by faith receive strength to apprehend the fullness of God. Remember Christ is in your faith. Hold faith, and you hold Christ.

If you know not how to get hold on faith, remember it is in the promise. Seek for a promise, and lay hold there. But perhaps you cry out, "I see the links of the chain so far off that, alas! I cannot take hold on the promise. I don't know which is for me; I cannot reach so far." Well, don't faint yet; there is another link still lower, that is to say, your wants. Can you be sure there is a wound within? Are you certain you are a sinner? Well then, reach your hand hither, "I came not to call the righteous, but sinners." Are you a helpless sinner? "To them who have no might, He increaseth strength." Are you an ungrateful, backsliding sinner? Hear Him say, "Thou hast played the harlot with many lovers; but return unto me saith the Lord."

If you doubt whether you may believe for a great measure of holiness; whether your soul, already in old age and barren, shall believe for abundant fruitfulness; answer yourself, my dear friend, from that word, "Whosoever will, let him come, and take of the water of life freely." I have just told Mrs. Smyth of one of your sisters here, once a deeper unbeliever than yourself, but now quite full of God. I refer you to her letter.

O my God, in mercy let Thy power rest on Thy dear servants! Convey, even by this poor scrawl, some power to their hearts—some fresh light into the mighty chain which begins with man's wickedness, hangs on God's mercy in the promises, is continued by faith and victory springing therefrom, and ends with Christ's fullness becoming all in all. We pray the God of love to be with your children, and all who meet with them. Tell sister Hammond to keep hold of the chain; it shall draw her into the holy of holies. With our kindest and most grateful remembrance of you both, we remain, your sincere but unworthy friends.

To Mr. Henry Brooke

Madeley, April 27th, 1784

My Dear Brother—Mercy, peace, and perfect love attend you, your dear partner, and the dear friends under your roof, with whom I beg you may abide under the cross, till, with John, Mary, and Salome, etc., you all can say, "We are crucified with Him, and the life we now live, we live by the faith of the Son of God, Who loved us and gave Himself for us.

You are certainly right when you prefer the inward to the outward. The former is the safer, but both together make up the beauty of holiness. The inward life may be compared to the husband, the outward to the fruitful wife. What God hath joined together let no man, nor even angel, put asunder.

With respect to the glory of the Lord: *it is at hand*, whatever false wisdom and unbelief may whisper to our hearts. It can be no farther off than the *presence* of Him Who fills all in all. Our wrong notions of things are a main hindrance to our stepping into it; and perhaps our minding more the cherubims of glory than the plain tables and the manna hid in the ark. "There is a passing," says Bromley, "from the outward to the inward, and from the inward to the inmost; and it is only from the inmost that we can see the Lord's spiritual glory." Pray, my dear brother, when you get so fixed in the inmost as not to lose sight of Him Who dwells in the light, and in the thick darkness, let me share your joy. Love will make me partake of your happiness.

With respect to what you say of the Kingdom coming with the outward pomp which is discoverable by the men of the world, it is strictly true. But that there is an inward display of power and glory under pentecostal Christianity is undeniable, both from our Lord's promises to His disciples, and from their experiences after the Kingdom was come to them with power. It is sometimes suggested to me that as the apostasy hath chiefly consisted in going after the pomp of the whore of Babylon, so that while the woman who fled into the wilderness remains there as a widow, she must be deprived even of those true ornaments and of that spiritual glory which was bestowed upon her on the day of Pentecost, the day of her espousals. I do not, however, close in with the suggestion, as I am not sure that it cannot come from Satan transformed into an angel of light, to rob me of a bright jewel of my Christian hope. To wait in deep resignation and with a constant attention to what the Lord will please to do or say concerning us and His Church, and to leave to Him the times and the seasons, is what I am chiefly called to do. I take care in the meanwhile of falling into either ditch—I mean into speculation which is careless of action, or into the activity which is devoid of spirituality. I would not have a lamp without oil, and I could not have oil without a lamp and a vessel to hold it in for myself, and to communicate it to others.

I thank you, my dear friend, for the books you have sent me. I read with great pleasure *Ramsay's Theological Works*, which were quite unknown to me. My good wishes attend both your brothers. Fare you well in Christ.

To James Ireland

Madeley, Sept. 13th, 1784

My Dear Friend—Surely the Lord keeps us both in slippery places, that we may still set loose to all below. Let us do so more and more, and make the best of those days which the Lord grants us to finish the work He has given us to do. O let us fall in with the gracious designs of His providence! Let us trim our lamps, gird our loins, and prepare to escape to the heavenly shore, as Paul did when he saw the leaky ship ready to go to the bottom, and made himself ready to swim to land.

I keep in my sentry box till Providence removes me. My situation is quite suited to my little strength. I may do as much or as little as I please, according to my weakness. And I have an advantage which I can have no where else in such a degree—my little field of action is just at my own door, so that if I happen to overdo myself, I have but a step from my pulpit to my bed, and from my bed to my grave.

I wish brother Tandy joy about opposition. This *must* be, and the more of it, the more will the word of God prevail. If I had a body full of vigor and a purse full of money, I should like well enough to travel about as Mr. Wesley does; but as Providence does not call me to it, I readily submit. The snail does best in its shell; were it to aim at galloping like the race horse, it would be ridiculous indeed. I thank God my wife, who joins me in thanks to you for your kind offer, is quite of my mind with respect to the call we have to a sedentary life. We are two poor invalids, who between us make *half* a laborer...

My dear partner sweetly helps me to drink the dregs of life, and to carry with ease the daily cross. Neither she nor I are long for this world; we see it, we feel it, and by looking at death and his Conqueror, we fight before hand our last battle with that last enemy whom our dear Lord hath overcome for us. That we may triumph over him with an humble, Christian courage is my prayer.

TO LADY MARY FITZGERALD

Madeley, Feb. 11th, 1785

HONORED AND DEAR MADAM—Mercy, righteousness, peace, and joy be multiplied to dear Lady Mary, and to all who are dear and near unto her, from the Father of mercies, through the Son of His boundless love, and through the Spirit of infinite love, which the Father breathes continually towards the Son, and the Son towards the Father! So prays John Fletcher. And who are we, my Lady, that we should not be swallowed up by this holy, loving, living Spirit which fills Heaven and earth? If we could exclude Him from our hearts, we might vilely set up *self* in opposition to Him Who is all in all. But whether we consider it or not, there He is, a true, holy, loving, merciful God. Assent to it, my Lady. Believe it. Rejoice in it. Let Him be God, all in all; your God in Christ Jesus; your Brother, Who is flesh of your flesh, bone of your bone; your Surety, Who payeth all your debt, in Whom the Father was reconciling you and us unto Himself, and in Whom we are accepted. What an ocean of love to swim in—to dive into! Don't be afraid to venture, and to plunge with all yours…

To Mr. Henry Brooke

Madeley, Feb. 28th, 1785

My Dear Brother—We are all shadows. Your mortal parent hath passed away, and we pass away after him. Blessed be the Author of every good and perfect gift for the shadow of His eternal paternity displayed to us in our deceased parents. What was good, loving, and lovely in them is hid with Christ in God, where we may enjoy it *implicitly*, and where we shall *explicitly* enjoy it when He shall appear.

A lesson I learn daily is to see things and persons in their *invisible root* and in their *eternal principle*, where they are not subject to change, decay, and death. There they blossom and shine in the primeval excellence allotted them by their gracious Creator. By this means I learn to walk by faith and not by sight. But, like a child, instead of walking straight and firm in this good spiritual way, I am still apt to cling here or there. This makes me cry, "Lord, let me see all things more clearly, that I may never mistake a shadow for the substance, nor put any creature—no not for a moment—in the place of the Creator, Who deserves to be loved, admired, and sought after with all the powers of our souls."

Tracing His image in all the footsteps of nature, or looking for the divine signature on every creature as we should look for the king's image on an old rusty medal, is true philosophy. And to find out that which is of God *in ourselves* is the true Wisdom—genuine godliness. I hope you will never be afraid nor ashamed of it. I see no danger in these studies and meditations, provided we still keep the end in view—the call of God, and the *shadowy nothingness* of all that is visible.

With respect to the great pentecostal display of the Spirit's glory, I still look for it within and without; and to look for it aright is the lesson I am learning. I am now led to be afraid of that in my nature which would be for pomp, show, and visible glory. I am afraid of falling by such an expectation into what I call spiritual judaizing—into a looking for Christ's coming in my own pompous conceit, which might make me reject Him if *His* wisdom, to crucify *mine*, chose to come in a meaner way; and if, instead of coming in His Father's glory, He chose to come meek, riding, not on the cherubim, but on the foal of an ass. Our Savior said, with respect to His going to the feast, "My time is not yet come." Whether His time to come and turn the thieves and buyers out of the outward Church is yet come, I know not. I doubt Jerusalem and the holy place are yet given to be trodden under foot by the Gentiles. But *my* Jerusalem! why it is not swallowed up of the glory of that which comes down from Heaven is a question which I wait to be solved by the teaching of the great Prophet Who is alone possessed of Urim and Thummim. The mighty power to wrestle with Him is all divine. I often pray,

That mighty faith on me bestow,
Which cannot ask in vain,
Which holds, and will not let Thee go,
Till I my suit obtain.
Till Thou into my soul inspire,
That perfect love unknown,
And tell my infinite desire,
Whate'er Thou wilt be done.

In short, the Lord crucifies my *wisdom* and my *will* every way; but I must be crucified as the thieves. All my bones must be broken, for there is still in me that impatience of wisdom which would stir when the tempter says, "Come down from the cross." It is not for us to know the times and seasons, the manner and mystical means of God's working; but only to hunger and thirst and lie passive before the Great Potter. In short, I begin to be content to be a vessel of clay or of wood, so I may be emptied of self and filled with my God, my all. Don't give up your confident hope; it saves still secretly, and hath a *present*, and, by and by, will have a *great* recompense of reward.

I am glad, exceeding glad, that your dear partner goes on simply and believingly. Such a companion is a great blessing, if you know how to make use of it. For when two of you shall agree touching one thing in prayer, it shall be done. My wife and I endeavor to fathom the meaning of that deep promise. Join your line to ours, and let us search what, after all, exceeds knowledge—I mean the wisdom and the power, the love and faithfulness of God.

My wife and I embrace you both. We pray you would help one another, and us, by your prayers. Adieu. "Be God's," as the French say; and see God yours in Christ, for you, and for all our dear brethren. We are your obliged servants.

To Mr. Melvill Horne

Madeley, May 10th, 1785

Dear Brother—I am sorry you should have been uneasy about the books. I received them safely, after they had lain for some time at Salop. I seldom look into any book but my Bible—not out of contempt, as if I thought they could not teach me what I do not know—but because "*Vita brevis, Ars longa.*"[1] I may never look into either of them again.

Go on improving yourself by reading, but above all by *meditation* and *prayer*. Allow our Lord to refine you in the fire of temptation. Where you see a lack, at home or abroad, within or without, look upon that lack as a warning to avoid the cause of

1 Life is short; art is long.

the leanness you perceive, and a call to secure the blessings which are ready to take their flight. Sometimes true riches, like those of this world, make themselves wings and flee away. The heavenly dove may be grieved and take its flight to humbler and more peaceful roofs.

I am glad you do not want hard or violent measures. I hope you never will countenance them, no not against what you dislike. I believe things will turn out very well at the Conference; and I shall be a witness of it, if the Lord of the harvest gives me a commission to be a spectator of the order and quietness of those who shall be there. If not, I shall help you by prayer to draw from far the blessing of love upon our friends.

In being moderate, humble, and truly desirous to be a Christian, that is, to be the least, the last, and the servant of all, we avoid running ourselves into difficulties, we escape many temptations, and many mortifying disappointments. For my part, as I expect nothing from men, they cannot disappoint me. And as I expect all good things from God in the time, way, measure, and manner it pleaseth Him to bestow, here I cannot be disappointed, because He does and will do all things well.

I trust you labor for God and souls, not for praise and self. When the latter are our aim, God, in mercy, blesses us with barrenness, that we may give up Barrabas, and release the humble Jesus, Whom we crucify afresh by setting the thief on the throne, and the Lord of glory at our footstool; for so do those who preach Christ out of contention, or that they may have the praise of men. That God may bless you and your labors is the prayer of your old brother.

TO MR. JAMES IRELAND

Madeley, July 19th, 1785

MY DEAR FRIEND—Blessed be God, we are still alive. In the midst of many infirmities we enjoy a degree of health spiritual and bodily. O how good was the Lord, to come as Son of Man to live here for us, and to come in His Spirit to live in us for ever! This is a mystery of godliness. The Lord make us full witness of it!

A week ago I was tried to the quick by a fever with which my dear wife was afflicted. Two persons whom she had visited having been carried off within a pistol shot of our house, I dreaded her being the third, but the Lord hath heard prayer and she is spared. O what is life! On what a slender thread hang everlasting things! However, my comfort is that this thread is as strong as the will of God and the word of His grace, which cannot be broken. That grace and peace, love and thankful joy may ever attend you, is the wish of your most obliged friends.

To Lady Mary Fitzgerald

Madeley, July 20th, 1785

Honored and Dear Lady—We have received your kind letter, and mournfully acquiesced in the will of our heavenly Father, Who by various infirmities and providences weans us from ourselves and our friends in order that we may be His without reserve. It was, perhaps, a peculiar mercy that Providence blocked up your way to this place this Summer. A bad Putrid Fever carries off several people in these parts. Two of our neighbors died of it last week; and my wife, who had visited them, was taken in so violent a manner that I was obliged to offer her up to God in good earnest, as an oblation worthy of a son of Abraham. I hope the worst is over, but her meekness will long preach to me, as well as my own. Dying people—we live in the midst of dying people. O let us live in sight of a dying, rising Savior, and the prospect of death will become first tolerable and then joyous. Or if we weep, as our Lord, at the grave of our friends, or at the side of their deathbeds, we shall triumph in hope that all will be for the glory of God and the good of our souls.

The Test of a New Creature

Or, Heads of Examination for Adult Christians

Examine yourselves, whether ye be in the faith (2 Cor. 13:5).

Whatever is the state of one wholly renewed must be, in a less degree, the state of all who are born from above. And whatever is the fruit of perfect holiness, to walk by the same rule must be the way to obtain the same salvation. The image of God is one, grace is the same, and to be in Christ is to believe, and have the fellowship of His Spirit.

Regeneration differs only in degrees of strength and soundness. In our early justification the divine life is comparatively small, and mixed with sin; but when perfectly renewed, we are strong and every part pure, holding, by faith, that salvation which makes us one with the Son of God. The law given in our first state and the law required by the Gospel, the covenant of works and the covenant of faith, are different. Whatever we see in the example of Jesus, and whatever He promises to bestow on His followers, are unquestionable privileges of Gospel salvation. Neither is the whole of this salvation—of our justification or of our renewal after the image of God—finished till the resurrection. Then we shall see Him as He is, and beholding Him face to face, His name shall be written on our foreheads. Nor can we ever have so much of the likeness of God as to be incapable of more; but rather the more we obtain of His image and favor, the more we are fitted to receive for ever and ever.

Heads of Examination

1. Do I feel any pride? or am I a partaker of the meek and lowly mind that was in Jesus? Am I dead to all desire of praise? If any

despise me, do I like them the worse for it? Or if they love and approve me, do I love them more on that account? Am I willing to be accounted useless and of no consequence—glad to be made of no reputation? Do humiliations give me real pleasure, and is it the language of my heart,

> "Make me little and unknown,
> Lov'd and priz'd by God alone"?

2. Does God bear witness in my heart that it is purified—that in all things I please Him?

3. Is the life I live, "by the faith of the Son of God," so that Christ dwelleth in me? Is Christ the life of all my affections and designs, as my soul is the life of my body? Is my eye single, and my soul full of light—all eye within and without—always watchful?

4. Have I always the presence of God? Does no cloud come between God and the eye of my faith? Can I rejoice evermore, pray without ceasing, and in every thing give thanks?

5. Am I saved from the fear of man? Do I speak plainly to all, neither fearing their frowns nor seeking their favors? Have I no shame of religion; and am I always ready to confess Christ, to suffer with His people, and to die for His sake?

6. Do I deny myself at all times, and take up my cross as the Spirit of God leads me? Do I embrace the cross of every sort, being willing to give up my ease and convenience to oblige others? Or do I expect them to conform to my hours, ways, and customs? Does the cross sit light upon me, and am I willing to suffer all the will of God? Can I trample on pleasure and pain? Have I

> "A soul inur'd to pain,
> To hardship, grief, and loss;
> Bold to take up, firm to sustain,
> The consecrated cross"?

7. Are my bodily senses and outward things all sanctified to me? Do I not seek my own things, to please myself? Do I seek

grace more for God than myself, preferring the glory of God to all in earth or Heaven—the Giver to the gift?

8. Am I poor in Spirit? Do I take pleasure in infirmities, in necessities, in distresses, in reproaches; so that out of weakness, want, and danger, I may cast myself on the Lord? Have I no false shame in approaching God? Do I seek to be saved, as a poor sinner, by grace alone?

9. Do I not lean to my own understanding? Am I ready to give up the point, when contradicted—unless conscience forbid—and am I easy to be persuaded? Do I esteem every one better than myself? Am I as willing to be a cipher as to be useful, and does my zeal burn bright notwithstanding this willingness to be nothing?

10. Have I no false wisdom, goodness, strength; as if the grace I feel were my own? Do I never take that glory to myself which belongs to Christ? Do I feel my want of Christ as much as ever, to be my all. And do I draw near to God, as poor and needy, only presenting before Him His well beloved Son? Can I say,

> "Every moment Lord I need
> The merit of Thy death.
> Still I'll hang upon my God,
> Till I Thy perfect glory see,
> Till the sprinkling of Thy blood
> Shall speak me up to Thee"?

Do I find joy in being thus nothing, empty, undeserving, giving all the glory to Christ? Or do I wish that grace made me something, instead of God all?

11. Have I meekness? Does it bear rule over all my tempers, affections, and desires; so that my hopes, fears, joy, zeal, love, and hatred are duly balanced? Do I feel no disturbance from others, and do I desire to give none? If any offend me, do I still love them and make it an occasion to pray for them? If condemned by the world, do I entreat? If condemned by the godly, am I one in whose mouth there is no reproof—replying only as conscience

and not as impatient nature dictates? If in the wrong, do I confess it? If in the right, do I submit (being content) to do well and suffer for it?

It is the sin of superiors to be overbearing, of inferiors to be stubborn. If, then, I am a servant, do I yield not only to the gentle but to the froward; committing my cause in silence to God? Or if a master, do I show all long suffering? The Lord of all was as He that serveth. If I am the greatest, do I make myself least and the servant of all? If a teacher, am I lowly, meek, and patient; not conceited, self-willed, nor dogmatic? Am I ready to give up the claims of respect due to age, station, parent, master, etc.? Or do I rigidly exact those demands?

12. Do I possess resignation? Am I content with whatever is or may be, seeing that God, the Author of all events, does, and will do, all for my good? Do I desire nothing but God, willing to part with all if the Lord manifest His will for my so doing? Do I know how to abound, and yet not gratify unnecessary wants? Being content with things needful, do I faithfully and freely dispose of all the rest for the help of others? Do I know how to suffer need? Is my confidence in God unshaken while I feel the distress of poverty and have the prospect of future want, while, humanly speaking, strangling were better than life? And in these circumstances, do I pity those who, having plenty, waste it in excess instead of helping me?

13. Am I just, doing all things as I would others should do unto me? Do I render due homage to those above me, not presuming on their lenity and condescension? As a superior, do I exercise no undue authority, taking no advantage of the timidity, respect, or necessity of any man? Do I consider the great obligation superiority lays me under of being lowly and kind and of setting a good example?

14. Am I temperate, using the world and not abusing it? Do I receive outward things in the order of God, making earth a scale to Heaven? Is the satisfaction I take in the creation consistent with my being dead to all below, and a means of leading me more to God? Is the turn of my mind and temper in due subjection,

not leading me to any extreme, either of too much silence or of too much talkativeness, of reserve or freedom?

15. Am I courteous, not severe; suiting myself to all with sweetness; striving to give no one pain, but to gain and win all for their good?

16. Am I vigilant, redeeming the time, taking every opportunity of doing good? Or do I spare myself, being careless about the souls and bodies to which I might do good? Can I do no more than I do? Do I perform the most servile offices—such as require labor and humiliation—with cheerfulness? Is my conversation always seasoned with salt, at every time administering some kind of savor to those I am with?

17. Do I love God with all my heart? Do I constantly present myself, my time, my substance, my talents, and all that I have, a living sacrifice? Is every thought brought into subjection to Christ? Do I like, or dislike, only such things as are pleasing or displeasing to God?

18. Do I love God with all my strength, and are my spiritual faculties always vigorous? Do I give way to sinful languor? Am I always on my watch? Do not business, worldly care, and conversation damp my fervor and zeal for God?

19. Do I love my neighbor as myself? Do I love every man for Christ's sake, and honor all men as the image of God? Do I think no evil, listen to no groundless surmises, nor judge from appearances? Can I bridle my tongue, never speaking of the fault of another but with a view to do good? And when I am obliged to do it, have I the testimony that I sin not? Have I that love which hopeth, believeth, and endureth all things?

20. How am I in my sleep? If Satan presents an evil imagination, does my will immediately resist, or give way to it?

21. Do I bear the infirmities of age or sickness without seeking to repair the decays of nature by strong liquors? Or do I make Christ my sole support, casting the burden of a feeble body into the arms of His mercy?

Many consider that perfect love, which casteth out fear, as instantaneous: all grace is so. But what is given in a moment is enlarged and established by diligence and fidelity. That which is instantaneous in its descent is perfective in its increase.

This is certain—too much grace cannot be desired or looked for. To believe and obey with all the power we have is the highway to receive all we have not. There is a day of Pentecost for believers, a time when the Holy Ghost descends abundantly. Happy they who receive most of this perfect love, and of that establishing grace which may preserve them from such falls and decays as they were before liable to.

Jesus, Lord of all, grant Thy purest gifts to every waiting disciple. Enlighten us with the knowledge of Thy will, and show us the mark of the prize of our high calling. Let us die to all Thou art not, and let us seek Thee with our whole heart, till we enjoy the fullness of the "purchased possession." Amen!

Miscellaneous Writings

On Seriousness

NOTHING is so contrary to godliness as levity. Seriousness consists in the matter of what is spoken, in the manner of speaking, in the dignity of behavior, and in weighty, not trifling actions. Some people are serious by nature, some by policy and for selfish ends, and some by grace and from a sense of duty.

Jesting and raillery, lightness of behavior, useless occupations, joy without trembling and awe of God, an affectation of vivacity and sprightliness, are all contrary to the Spirit of God. "A fool laughs loud," saith Solomon, "but a wise man scarce smiles a little."

Levity is contrary to contrition and self knowledge, to watching and prayer, frequently to charity and to common sense, when death is at our heels. Levity is also destructive of all devotion—in our own heart and in that of others—by unfitting the company for receiving good, and bringing a suspicion of hypocrisy upon all.

Seriousness is useful to prevent the foregoing miscarriages, to keep grace, to recommend piety and a sense of God's presence, to leave room for the Spirit to work, and to check levity and sin in others. And have we not motives sufficient to seriousness? Are we not priests and kings to God—temples of the Holy Ghost? Are we not walking in the presence of God—on the verge of the grave—and in sight of eternity?

All who walk with God are serious, taking their Lord for their example, and walking by Scripture precepts and warnings.

"But are we to renounce innocent mirth?" Our souls are diseased. "Are we to be dull and melancholy?" Seriousness and solid happiness are inseparable. "Is there not a time for all things?" There is no time for sin and folly.

On Pleasure

DYING to pleasure, even the most innocent, we shall live to God. Of pleasures there are four sorts: (1) Sensual pleasures—of the eye, ear, taste, smell, ease, indulgence, etc. (2) Pleasures of the heart—attachments, entanglements, creature love, unmortified friendships. (3) Pleasures of the mind—curious books, deep researches, speculations, hankerings after news, wit, fine language. (4) Pleasures of the imagination—schemes, fancies, suppositions.

God requires that we should deny ourselves in all these respects because (1) God will have the heart, which He cannot have if pleasure hath it; and God is a jealous God. (2) There is no solid union with God until, in a Christian sense, we are dead to creature comforts. Pleasure is the Gordian knot. (3) God is purity; hankering after pleasures is the cause of almost all our sins—the bait of temptation. (4) God calls us to show our faith and love by a spirit of sacrifice. Pleasure is Isaac. (5) Denying ourselves, hating our life, dying daily, crucifying the flesh, putting off the old man, are Gospel precepts—so is cutting off the right hand, plucking out the right eye, and forsaking all to follow Christ. (6) God makes no exceptions. All the offending members must be cut off; every leak must be stopped, or the corrupting pleasure spared gets more ascendant. (7) Pleasures render the soul incapable of the operations of the Spirit, and obstruct divine consolations.

Now nature is all for pleasure, and lives upon sensuality. The senses, heart, mind, and imagination pursue always objects that may gratify them. We love pleasure so as to deprive ourselves of every thing to enjoy it in some kind or other. And we undergo hardships to procure it. Nature frets horribly if disappointed in this favorite pursuit; and yet if nature is pampered, grace must be starved.

Earthly pleasures are of a corrupting nature. For example, that of taste, if indulged, spreads through, corrupts, and dissipates all the powers of the soul and body. It is so much the more dangerous as it hides itself under a mask of necessity, or color of lawfulness, and does all the mischief of a concealed traitor. It betrays with a kiss, poisons with honey, wounds in its smiles, and kills while it promises happiness.

Indulgence enervates and renders us incapable of suffering from God, men, devils, or self. It stands continually in the way of our doing, as well as suffering, the will of God. It is much easier, therefore, to fly from pleasure than to remain within due bounds in its enjoyment. The greatest saints find nothing so difficult, nothing makes them tremble so, as the use of pleasure; for it requires the strictest watchfulness and the most vigorous attention. He must walk steadily who can walk safely on the brink of a precipice.

The absolute necessity of dying to pleasure will appear from the following considerations. The earthly senses must be spiritualized. The sensual heart must be purified. The wandering mind must be fixed. The foolish imagination must be made sober.

Worldly pleasures are all little, low, and transitory, and a hindrance to our chief good. Much moderation, however, is to be used in the choice and degree of our mortifications. Through pride, nature often prompts us to great extremes, which hurt the body, and sometimes lead the mind into sourness and obstinacy. But to know and walk in the right path of self denial, we have need of much recollection.

On Hypocrisy

MANY pretend to a share of the holy child, but we need all the wisdom of the true Solomon to know the mother from the harlot. An hypocrite hides wickedness under a cloak of goodness: clouds without rain, wells without water, trees without fruit, the ape of piety, the mask of sin, glorious without—carrion within. They do not put off, but throw a cloak over it.

Satan an Arch-hypocrite

Having apostasized from God himself, he endeavored to vent his malice and envy on God's favorite—man. He disguised himself as a serpent, showed much love and friendship, and by that appearance deceived Eve. Though God has prepared an antidote, yet he goes about murdering the children of men with increasing craft (for he is now the old serpent). He is still opposing Christ, picking up the seed of the word, hindering the sowers, sowing tares. He is the strong man, armed with the force of an angel, the subtlety of a fallen angel, able to insinuate himself into souls as into serpents. His baits are pleasure for the sensual, wealth for the muckworm, honor for the ambitious, and science for the curious. In each he transforms himself as an angel of light, gilding all with heavenly appearances; but his light is darkness—and how great is that darkness!

He works admirably on predisposition. (1) On ignorance of evil, or forgetfulness of the sword of the Spirit. He finds us blind, or blinds our eyes to make us turn the better in his mill. (2) On security. He puts far from us the thoughts of death—"Ye shall not surely die." (3) On idleness. When David was idle at home, and Joab in the field, Satan took that opportunity to draw him into the snare of lust. (4) On unreasonable scruples of conscience—discouragement—extremes. If he can't put out the fire of zeal, he will make it break out at the chimney, and drive fasting into starving. (5) He suits his temptations to the subjects, drives the nail that will go, and causes the stream of natural propensities to flow. He tempts not, in general, the old to pleasure, nor the young to covetousness, nor the sick to drunkenness, but to impatience.

The Moral Hypocrite

Many mistake nature for grace, and so rest short of a true change. Strong sense, keen wit, lively parts, and a good natural temper puff up many. The tempering makes a vast difference in many blades, all made of the same metal; some of which will bend before they break, others break before they bend. Good nature, without grace, maketh a fairer show than grace with an evil nature. A cur outruns a greyhound with a clog.

The hypocrite derives his honor from his birth, the child of God from his new birth. The hypocrite hath his perfections from the body—from his complexion and constitution, which are not praiseworthy; but the Christian hath them from his inner part—the soul. A warm temper hath often the appearance of zeal, a cooler of patience, melancholy of contemplation, lively blood and strong spirits of spiritual joy.

The hypocrite serves God with what costs him nothing, only going down the stream; but the Christian works with strife and industry, wrestleth, and keeps his body under.

The hypocrite is disposed to some virtues, and refrains from those vices that are contrary to his taste and humor, as an elephant abhors a mouse; but the Christian shuts every door against sin and is thoroughly furnished to every good work.

The hypocrite puts reason in the place of religion. On the contrary, the Christian brings reason under the command of religion. His understanding bows to faith, and his free will to God's free grace.

The hypocrite derives his virtues from himself, spider like. "Cursed be the man that trusteth in man" (Jer. 17:5). The Christian hath his virtues from above. The one is like marshy ground, the other is watered from Heaven. Again, the hypocrite curses himself by giving to reason the command of appetite, not knowing that his reason is crooked; but the Christian puts all under the strict rule of grace. Grace is Sarah; Reason is Agar. The one talks of right reason, the other rectifieth it.

The hypocrite puts honesty in the place of piety; but the Christian is honest and kind from a principle of genuine piety. There was a difference between Alexander and David pouring out water—the one before his soldiers, the other before the Lord.

He hath for virtues only shining vices—virtues proceeding from unsanctified reason, and spoiled by the intention. Thus a covetous, indolent man avoids and hates law suits. He is sober and temperate through love of money or of health and reputation. He is diligent and industrious to compass profit. But the Christian hath the truth, if he lacks the perfection of virtue. The one shines as rotten wood, the other as gold in the ore.

The hypocrite cries up virtue and exclaims against vice rather by speech than practice; but the king's daughter is glorious within. The one speaks, the other lives, great things.

The hypocrite keeps himself from gross sins, but harbors spiritual corruptions. Does he subdue his passions? They are in the way of his glory and quiet. Does he do good? It is to be more in love with himself. The Christian cleanseth himself from all spiritual vices. The one is settled on the lees of self love, the other is emptied of self and filled with Christ.

The hypocrite compares himself with the child of God when under disadvantages; as for example, when he is fallen or overtaken in an infirmity. But the whitest devil shall not stand in the judgment with the most tawny child of God. The meteor may blaze, but the star standeth.

The Hearing Hypocrite

The hearing hypocrite hears Christ's word without benefit. He assembles with the pious, whom he deceives, as he hopes to deceive Christ (Luke 13:26). He goes to meet Christ, not as the bride, but only as the bride's friend. He is the stony ground. He is sermon proof, repels conviction, takes nothing to himself, or shakes it off as sheep do the rain. He hath the forehead of the whore (Jer. 3:3), and refuses to be ashamed. Christ condemns him, both as a worker of iniquity, and a builder on the sand. The Christian hears, so that his profiting appears unto all men. He hears Christ Himself through the minister. And the word is able to save his soul, as a savor of life unto life. Nor is he a forgetful hearer, but a doer of the word.

The hypocrite will hear only such ministers as suit his humor. Balaam suits Balak, and a lying prophet Ahab. He will neglect or slight others. The Christian hears God's voice through every messenger of His, the plainer the message the better he receives the message—"as an angel of God, even as Christ Jesus" (Gal. 4:14). He judges not of the word by the preacher, but of the preacher by the word. He, like Jehoshaphat, will hear Micaiah preach, rather than the 400 prophets of Baal.

The hypocrite hears in hopes of hearing something new; therefore, when he has heard a few times, he grows weary and longs for a new preacher. An unsanctified heart, like a sick stomach, loathes its daily bread. But the Christian is never tired of the sincere milk of the word. He desires no new wine. He likes manna after forty years—"Evermore give us this bread."

The hypocrite hearkens more after eloquence than substance. He likes Apollos, not Christ's messenger. He hears not for life. He sports with the infirmities of Sampson—but death is at the door. The Christian looks most to the power of the word. He comes not as to a show, but to the bar. He weighs the matter rather than the manner, and regards the message more than the messenger. The one falls down before man, the other before God.

He will not hear all. Comforts, promises, and general truths he loves; the doctrine of the cross he hates. A foil, a wooden sword that draws no blood suits him. The Christian hears all God's word, and loves to be smitten. He does not say, "Hast thou found me, O mine enemy?" but, "Search me and try my heart."

The hypocrite looks on the word as a story or a landscape. He loves to hear of Christ's miracles, of the prodigal son, etc., but draws a curtain before his own picture. The Christian looks on the word as a glass to see himself. The one uses the word as children their books, looking more at the pictures than the lesson. The other sees himself and improves.

He hears without preparing his heart to hear. He minds his outward more than his inward man. He uses no exercise to get an appetite. It is enough if he hears, though he digests nothing. He sows among thorns, having never ploughed, and they choke all. The Christian looks to his feet, comes hungry to the house of God, longing to be fed, and is not willing to go without his portion.

He hears only for the present time, as he would hear a concert of music. The Christian hears both for the time present and to come. He studies what he hears, and to the end that he may turn it in to practice. He remembers that word, "Take heed how you hear."

He proposes to himself some carnal end—if any at all—as to be noticed for his diligence, to be reputed a good churchman, to fulfil his task of hearing, perhaps to cavil and find fault, to make amends for not doing, to please a friend. Festus thus pleased Agrippa, and Ahab heard Micaiah for Jehoshaphat's sake. But the Christian hears for his own and others' edification.

If the hypocrite is of the second class of hearers, he sometimes pretends to practice as an excuse for not hearing. "I have," says he, "enough in one sermon to practice all the week." The Christian makes hearing and practice go hand in hand. He will redeem time for hearing from recreation and sleep. His hearing is a spur to his practice. He does not pretend practice as a hindrance to his hearing, like Judas, who, out of pretended regard to the poor, sought to rob Christ of His due.

Sometimes he trembleth under the word, but yet he shifts it off before it has taken hold of his heart. As a tree shaken by the wind takes deeper root, so is he more rooted in his sins. Felix's fearfulness surpriseth the hypocrite before he is aware. He is ashamed of himself, angry at the preacher, and, Cain like, he runs from God instead of going to Him. But the Christian trembles at the word as afraid to sin against it. One is Pharaoh, the other Josiah.

He is a seeming friend, but a secret foe, to the Gospel. When the word is a hammer, he is an anvil. When it is a fire, he is clay. But the Christian is both reconciled to, and transformed into the word, receiving it as the word of God in the love thereof. If the word be a nail, it nails him to Christ; if a sword, he loves to be cut and dissected; if a fire, he is like water or as gold. The one kisses the word, like Judas; the other embraces it, as Joseph did Benjamin.

The Praying Hypocrite

The praying hypocrite prays with his tongue but not with his heart. The heart of the Christian goes first in prayer. The hypocrite asks according to his wishes, looking no farther, like Israel for quails, Balaam for leave to curse God's people, Rachel for children. But the Christian is like Hannah, who prayed hard and submitted all to God.

He is wavering, and double-minded. "Can God furnish a table in the wilderness?" "Will He hear and answer?" The Christian asketh in faith, nothing wavering—as Moses at the Red Sea, while Israel cried and expected death.

The hypocrite is sometimes presumptuous also: "Wherefore have I fasted, and Thou seest not?" The Christian always comes as a poor beggar, crying with the Centurion, "I am not worthy." The hypocrite quarrelleth with God if not answered: "This evil is of the Lord." But the Christian waiteth patiently, saying, "It is the Lord, let Him do as He pleaseth."

He prays without repentance, regarding iniquity in his heart; but the Christian confesses and forsakes his sin. The hypocrite prays without faith, without expecting an answer; therefore he often cuts short his prayer—especially in secret. The Christian pours out his soul in prayer—gives good measure, pressed down, running over, being assured that that word standeth fast: "If ye, being evil, know how to give good gifts unto your children, how much more shall my heavenly Father give His Holy Spirit to them that ask Him?"

At other times the hypocrite will exceed measure—but only in company, like the Ave Maria's of the Papists. The true Christian measures his prayers by his affections, and by works of charity and duty.

The hypocrite prays in adversity, not in prosperity. He comes like the leper or beaten child. The Christian, as the loving son, prays in prosperity, without the compulsion of the rod. Or, perhaps, he will pray in prosperity, but in adversity his heart sinks, like Nabal's. He murmurs, complains, and cries out, "Why doth the Lord do thus unto me?" The Christian remembers those words of St. James, "Is any afflicted, let him pray." The one, as a bastard, runs away. The other kisses the rod and sees everything as the answer of prayer, submitting himself wholly to the will of God.

The Preaching Hypocrite Worse Than All

Admitted of men, not called of God, he preaches Christ, but not for Christ. "Put me," saith he, "into the priest's office, that I may eat a morsel of bread." He is, perhaps, a preacher of righteousness, but a worker of iniquity. But the true Christian preacher only spends and is spent upon Christ and His interest. He is careful not only of His gifts, but of His grace; not only to be sent of men, but of God. The one preaches himself and for himself, the other preaches Christ and for Christ.

The hypocrite is ambitious to show his learning—to be admired rather than to be useful. Not so St. Paul (1 Cor. 2). A scribe well instructed bringeth out of his own treasures things new and old. He brings in learning, but not divine learning. His artificial fire hath no warmth in it. But the Christian minister, though perhaps learned in Egyptian wisdom as Moses, and in Greek literature as St. Paul, who quoted Aratus to the Athenians (Acts 17:28), Menander to the Corinthians (1 Cor. 15:33), Epimenides to Titus (Tit. 1:12), never uses it but as the Agar of Sarah, Christ crucified being his chief knowledge.

The hypocrite uses divine learning to human, carnal ends—to

get preferment or fame, to support opinions or parties. The minister of Christ handles not the word of God deceitfully, but by manifestation of the truth (2 Cor. 4:2). He glorieth not in his preaching, a necessity being laid upon him by Christ.

The hypocrite chooses subjects on which he may shine and please. The other chooses those which may awaken and edify, disclaiming men pleasing. The one shoots over the heads, the other aims at the hearts of his hearers, suiting himself to the meanest capacity.

He puts on a face of zeal, without zeal, and, trying to move others, is himself unmoved. He cannot say with Christ, "The zeal of thine house hath eaten me up." His zeal is an *ignis fatuus*,[2] or perhaps a heathenish fire lighted at Seneca's torch—not a burning as well as a shining light. He may have some feelings, but they are over with his sermon or prayer; some warmth for the church, as Jehu, because it is his party. But the Christian minister hath more zeal in his bosom than on his tongue. Elijah-like, the word of the Lord is as a fire in his bones. His soul mourns in secret places for the sins he reproves openly (Jer. 13:17). He can put "*probatum est*" to what he preaches, and his zeal hath a very large measure of Gospel love. It saves others while it consumes himself.

The hypocrite, perhaps strict in his rules, loose in his practice, binds heavy burdens that he toucheth not himself. He is like a finger post, which shows the way but never walks in it. He promises liberty while he is himself the slave of sin. The true preacher is afraid to preach what he practices not—he lives his sermons over. As a brave captain, he saith, "Follow me." He aims at Thummim as well as Urim, perfection as well as light.

The one makes the way to Heaven as broad as he can—at least to himself—and oft times allows things to others to screen himself. The other makes the way to Heaven narrower to himself than to his hearers, and never gives up the least of the word lest his own foot should be pinched.

2 alternately called will-o'-the-wisp, or Jack o'lantern.

On Lukewarmness

THE lukewarm are of two sorts. The first will speak against enormities but plead for little sins—will go to church and sacrament, but also to plays, races, and shows—will read the Bible, and also romances and trifling books. They will have family prayer, at least on Sundays, but after it unprofitable talk, evil speaking, and worldly conversation. They plead for the church, yet leave it for a card party, a pot companion, or the fireside. They think they are almost good enough, and they who aim at being better are (to be sure) hypocrites. They are under the power of anger, evil desire, and anxious care. But they suppose that all men are the same, and talk much of being saved by true repentance and doing all they can. They undervalue Christ, extol morality and good works, and do next to none. They plead for old customs. They will do as their fathers did, though ever so contrary to the word of God. Whatever hath not custom to plead for it, though ever so much recommended in Scripture, is accounted by them a heresy. They are greatly afraid of being too good, and of making too much ado about their souls and eternity. They will be sober, but not enthusiasts. The Scriptures they quote most and understand least are: "Be not righteous over much;" "God's mercies are over all His works;" "There is a time for all things," etc. They call themselves by the name of Christ, but worship Baal.

The second sort of lukewarm persons assent to all the whole Bible, talk of repentance, faith, and the new birth, commend holiness, plead for religion, use the outward means, and profess to be and to do more than others. But they yield to carelessness, self indulgence, fear of man, dread of reproach, and of loss, hatred of the cross, love of ease, and the false pleasures of a vain imagination. These say, do, and really suffer many things; but they rest short of the true change of heart, the one thing needful being still lacking. They are as the foolish virgins, without oil—as the man not having on the wedding garment.

Of these the Lord hath said, "He will spew them out of His mouth." But why so severe a sentence? Because, (1) Christ will have a man hearty and true to his principles. He looks for truth in the inward parts. As a consistent character He commended even the unjust steward. (2) Religion admits of no lukewarmness, and it is by men of this character that His name is blasphemed. (3) A bad servant is worse than a careless neighbor; and a traitor in the guise of a friend is more hateful and more dangerous than an open enemy. Judas was more infamous than Pilate. (4) The cold having nothing to trust to, and harlots and publicans, enter into the Kingdom of Heaven before moral or evangelical pharisees who, in different degrees, know their Master's will and do it not. "They shall be beaten with many stripes."

Union with Christ

Thou wilt keep him in perfect peace, whose mind is stayed on Thee: because he trusteth in Thee (Isa. 26:3).

THE very center of Christian religion is union with Christ and the receiving Him as our all; in other words called faith, or a staying our minds on Him. To the doing this there are many hindrances, but the two greatest and most general ones are:

First, The want of self-knowledge. This keeps ninety-nine out of one hundred from Christ. They know not, or rather feel not, that they are blind, naked, leprous, helpless, and condemned; that all their works can make no atonement, and that nothing they can do will fit them for Heaven. When this is truly known, the first grand hindrance to our union with Christ is removed.

The second is, The want of understanding the Gospel of Christ—the want of feeling therein the firm foundation given us for this pure and simple faith, the only solid ground of staying our souls on God. We must remember that the Gospel is good news, and not to be slow of heart to believe it. Christ receiveth sinners. He undertaketh their whole concern. He giveth not only repentance, but remission of sins and the gift of the Holy Ghost. He creates them anew. His love makes the bride and then delights in her. The want of viewing Christ in this light, as the Author and Finisher of our salvation, hinders the poor humble penitent from casting himself wholly on the Lord, although He hath said, "Cast thy burden on the Lord, and He shall sustain thee."

I do not mention sin, for sin is the very thing which renders man the object of Christ's pity. Our sins will never turn away the heart of Christ from us, for they brought Him down from Heaven to die in our place. And the reason why iniquity separates between God and our souls is because it turns our eyes from Him and shuts up in us the capacity of receiving those beams of love which are ever descending upon and offering themselves to us. But sin sincerely lamented and brought by a constant act of faith and prayer before the Lord shall soon be consumed, as the thorns laid close to a fire. Only let us abide thus waiting, and the Lord will pass through them and burn them up together.

When the soul feels its own helplessness and receives the glad tidings of the Gospel, it ventures upon Christ. And though the world, the flesh, and the devil pursue, so that the soul seems often to be on the brink of ruin, it has still only to listen to the Gospel and venture on Christ, as a drowning man on a single plank, with "I can but perish," remembering these words, "Thou wilt keep him in perfect peace, whose mind is stayed on Thee, because he trusteth in Thee."

The consequence of thus trusting is that God keeps the soul from its threefold enemy—defends it in temptation, in persecution, in heaviness. Through all, it finds power to repose itself on Christ—to say, "God shall choose my inheritance for me." Here the Christian finds peace with God, peace with himself, and peace with all around him—the peace of pardon, the peace of holiness; for both are obtained by staying the mind on Christ. He walks in the perpetual recollection of a present God, and is not disturbed by anything. If he feels sin, he carries it to the Savior; and if in heaviness through manifold temptations, he still holds fast his confidence—he is above the region of clouds.

The careless sinner is not to be exhorted to trust in Christ; it would be to cast pearls before swine. Before an act of faith, there must be an act of self-despair. Before filling there must be emptiness. Is this thy character? Then suffer me to take away thy false props. Upon what dost thou stay thy soul? Thy honesty, morality, humility, doing good, using the means, business, friends, confused thoughts of God's mercy? This will never do. Thou must be brought to say, "What shall I do to be saved?" Without trembling at God's word thou canst not receive Christ. Nothing short of love will do.

The penitent needs, and blessed be God has, every encouragement. You have nothing but sin—it is time you should understand the Gospel. You see yourself sinking—Christ is with you.

You despair of yourself—hope in Christ. You are overcome—Christ conquers. Self condemned—He absolves. Why do you not believe? Is not the messenger, the word, the Spirit of God, sufficient? You want a joy unspeakable—the way to it is by thus waiting patiently upon God. Look to Jesus. He speaks peace. Abide looking, and your peace shall flow as a river.

Holy Violence

The Kingdom of Heaven suffereth violence, and the violent take it by force (Matt. 11:12).

THE grand device of Satan is to prevent us from seeing the necessity of this holy violence, or from putting it in execution. To prevent the effect of this stratagem our blessed Lord gives us the plainest directions in these words, "Strive to enter in at the strait gate." "Labor for the meat that endureth to eternal life," etc., etc. But in no Scripture is the direction made more plain than in that of the text (Matt. 11:12). Let us consider I. The nature of this Kingdom. II. How the violent take it by force. III. Answer an objection to the doctrine of the text.

This Kingdom is that of grace, which brings down a heavenly nature and felicity into the believing soul. The Kingdom within us is "righteousness, and peace, and joy." It is Jesus apprehended by faith, as given for us, and felt by love, as living in us. In a word, it is the image of God lost in Adam and restored by Christ—pardon, holiness, and happiness, issuing in eternal glory.

This Kingdom suffereth violence, which is offered (1) To those lords who reign over us—the world, the devil, the flesh. These rebels must be turned out. Our own wills must be overcome, and ourselves surrendered up to God as to our lawful and chosen Sovereign. (2) An humble, holy, sacred violence must be used in prayer—with Jesus, that He would open in our hearts the power of faith, apply the efficacy of His blood, and bestow upon us the spirit of prayer; or in other words, the prayer of faith—with the Father, that He would look through the pillar of fire and discomfit all our enemies—with the Holy Ghost, that He would take up His abode with us.

Of this violence we have an example in Jacob wrestling with the Angel, Who said, "Let Me go, for the day breaketh;" and he said, "I will not let thee go, till Thou bless me" (Gen. 11:26). Here Jacob, being left alone, improves his solitude. Danger and trouble work in him the right way. He prays, prays earnestly, and that against much discouragement. God and man seem to oppose him, for the Angel of the Covenant wrestled as if to get loose from his hold. It was a spiritual wrestling. He wept and made supplication, but before he prevails the Angel touched the hollow of Jacob's thigh, and hindered him from wrestling in his own strength. Then the Spirit alone made intercession. Nature failed and grace was conqueror. "When I am weak, then am I strong."

He says, "Let Me go," as God once said to Moses, "Let Me alone." Thus does the Lord sometimes try our faith. This was the case of the woman of Canaan, when Jesus at first answered her not, and afterwards said, "It is not meet to take the children's bread and cast it to the dogs." But when she still worshipped, prayed, and waited, she obtained these words of approbation, "O woman, great is thy faith!" as well as the answer of her prayer. So the Angel saith, "Let me go, for the day breaketh"—thy affairs want thee—thou must have rest. But Jacob foregoes all for the blessing—rest, family, weariness, pain. He answers, "I will not let Thee go, unless Thou bless me." So must it be with us. None prevail but those who take the Kingdom by violence. He conquers at last.

"What is thy name?" saith God. He will have the sinner know himself and confess what he is. Then He gives the new name, "A prince with God." If God be for us, who can be against us? The Angel does not tell him His name, for the tree of life is better than the tree of knowledge. He saw God face to face and lived. So is it with faithful wrestlers. God resists only to increase our desires, and we must be resolved to hearken to nothing that would hinder. Weariness, care, friends, fear, and unbelief must all be thrown aside when we seek to see God face to face, and to be brought into the light of life.

They who are weary of the Egyptian yoke of outward and inward sin, who cannot rest without the love of Jesus, the life of God, at last become violent. They forcibly turn from the world. By force they attack the devil, bring themselves by force before God, and drag out, by strong confession, the evils that lurk within.

Against these they fight, by detesting and denying them. Their strength is in crying mightily to the Lord, and expecting continually that fire which God will rain from Heaven upon them. All this must be done by force and with great conflicts; for it is against nature, which hath the utmost reluctance to it.

The words of the text allude to the taking a fortified town by storming it, and this is of all military expeditions the most dangerous. The enemy is covered and hid, and those who scale the walls have nothing but their arms and courage. But can the wrestling soul overcome? can he take this Kingdom? Ah no, not by his own strength; but his Joshua will take it for him. God only requires that we should entreat Him to do this. The prayer of repentance and the prayer of faith storm Mount Zion, the city of God. He that is violent shall receive the Kingdom of God—justification and sanctification. But remember, the violent take it by force. He shall have many a hard struggle with God's enemies, and, it may be, many with the Lord Himself, before He declares him conqueror.

Some object, "We have no might, and to endeavor to take the Kingdom by violence is taking the matter out of God's hand. Is it not better to wait for the promise, to stand still and see the salvation of God?" If you mean by "standing still," not agonizing to enter in at the strait gate, not wrestling in prayer and fighting the good fight of faith—may God save you from this stillness! You err, not knowing the Scriptures. The standing still there recommended is to possess your soul in patience without dejection, fear, and murmuring. Stand still as the apostles, who watched together in prayer, ran with patience the race set before them, and fought manfully, as faithful soldiers, under the banner of the cross. Any other stillness is of the devil and leads to his kingdom.

Search the New Testament and show me one standing still after he had been convinced of his needs. Did the Centurion? Did the woman of Canaan? Did blind Bartimeus stand still? Did St. Paul? Did the woman with the bloody issue stand still? Did not all of them use the power they had? I do not desire you to use what you have not; only be faithful stewards of the manifold grace entrusted to you. A Kingdom, a Kingdom of Heaven is before you—power to reign with Jesus as His priests and kings. Stir up then thy faith. Reach forward to the things which are before. Become a wrestling Jacob, and you shall shortly be a prevailing Israel. Be not discouraged, for as a good man observes, "God frequently gives in one moment what He hath apparently withheld for many years."

Christ's Agony in the Garden

And being in an agony He prayed more earnestly: and His sweat was as it were great drops of blood falling down to the ground (Luke 22:44).

Many desire to know what passes in the heart of great men when under afflicting circumstances or engaged in some great undertaking. Behold the most sublime scene of suffering held out to us in the word of God. Here are laid open the last, the dying thoughts and cruel sufferings of the Savior of mankind. Here is a scene in which we are all most deeply interested. Let us look into: I. The agony of our Savior. II. What He did in His agony. III. The amazing consequences of that agony.

The agony of our Lord was a conflict—a violent struggle—a grappling and wrestling with the deepest horror—the agitation of a breast penetrated with the greatest sense of fear and amazement. "He was heard in that He feared."

The cause of His agony was: (1) The powers of darkness—legions of devils—who poured on His devoted head their utmost rage and malice. Every wound which sin had given and the devil had power to inflict, the pure and naked bosom of Jesus opened itself to receive. The prince of darkness, whose chain was let loose for the purpose, now ruled His hour and, to appearance, triumphed over the Prince of life. (2) The feeling of the weight of the wrath of God (and who knoweth the power of His wrath?) as kindled against sin—the terrors of the Lord—the cup of trembling—the withdrawing of God's comfortable presence. (3) The fear of His farther sufferings—a violent, dreadful, and approaching death. (4) The atoning for our coldness, and the painful foresight of how truly those words of the prophet might be applied to many, "Is it nothing to you, all ye that pass by?"

During His agony He prayed more earnestly. He prayed earnestly before, but now more earnestly. Before, He kneeled; but now He threw Himself prostrate on the earth. He prayed aloud with strong cries and tears (Heb. 5:7). He was in an agony, every power of soul and body being stretched to the utmost. Those who seldom or never pray are strangers to spiritual conflicts.

The greatness of His agony and intenseness of His prayer caused that amazing circumstance of His sweat being as it were great drops of blood. Amazing! Because it was a cold, damp night He lay on the ground. It was so profuse as to run down in great drops to the ground. The sweat was mixed with blood, bursting out of the capillary vessels through the open pores.

Observe, Adam sinned in a garden; in a garden Christ expiates sin. Before death, "In the sweat of thy brow, etc." before death Christ sweat, and with all His body labored. "In sorrow shalt thou bring forth." Christ sweat blood—strong sign of pain. "Cursed is the ground, etc." Christ, when made sin and a curse, lies prostrate on the ground and bedews it with blood.

Brethren, we must all be brought to an agony; yea, we must be Crucified with Christ if we would reign with Him. Beware then of vilifying the spiritual agonies of the children of God by calling them mad fits.

You who in agony have brought forth children, or struggled under the load of excessive drinking, or labored for life when in danger—struggle and agonize now for your souls.

Learn to pray most when most troubled—when weakest—when most tempted. Still look to the Lord Jesus—adore Him—love Him. Be not dry, like Gideon's fleece, in the midst of this sacred dew. O come for the answer of His prayer. It is thy balm of Gilead, the precious ointment which runs down to the skirts of His clothing. Wash away thy sin. Bathe in His bloody sweat; it is the former and the latter rain, bedewing prophets and apostles.

Let every believer remember (and rejoice in the remembrance) that sweat, pain, the earth, the grave, are sanctified. And let every stubborn unbeliever beware of the cry of His blood. It now cries better things—by and by it will cry bitterer things—than the blood of Abel.

The Rich Fool[3]

Thou fool, this night thy soul shall be required of thee (Luke 12:20).

LET us consider, 1. Why our Lord calls the person mentioned in the text a fool: "Thou fool." 2. The sudden and unexpected separation between this rich man and his all. 3. Make some observations on the nature and value of a soul. 4. Observe who shall require the rich man's soul: "It shall be required." 5. Make some remarks on the last words of the text: "Thy soul shall be required of thee."

1. It is not without good reason that our Lord addressed the rich man in the text with "Thou fool." The picture our Lord has drawn of him hath eight strokes, each of which proves this worldling to have been an egregious fool.

(a) He was rich in this world, but neglected being rich towards God—rich in grace.

(b) He was perplexed without reason, and exclaimed, "What shall I do? I have not where to bestow my fruits." Had he been wise, he would rather have cried out with the jailor, "What shall I do to be saved?" Or he would have enquired whether all the houses of his poor neighbors were full, and whether he could not bestow upon them some of those fruits the abundance of which made him so uneasy.

(c) He determined to "pull down his barns"—not to break off his sins. The pile of them, though towering to Heaven like Babel, did not make him uneasy.

(d) He resolved to build greater barns, but forgot to build the hopes of his salvation on the rock of ages (Matt. 8:24).

(e) He would say to his soul, "Soul, thou hast goods laid up." But had he been wise he would have considered that, although he was rich as to his outward circumstances and the things which support the body, yet his soul was poor, miserable, blind, and naked (Rev. 3:17).

3 This article is slightly abridged from the original.

(f) He had the folly to promise himself a long life, as if he had a lease of it, signed by his heavenly Lord. "Soul," said he, "thou hast much goods laid up for many years." But God said, "Thou fool, this night…"

(g) He would say to his soul, "Soul, take thine ease." But had he been directed by wisdom, he would have exhorted his soul not to rest till he had obeyed the apostle's precept, "Work out your own salvation with fear and trembling" (Phil. 2:12). Alas! how common and how dangerous is the mistake of the children of this world, who openly follow this fool and say either to themselves or to one another, "Soul, take thine ease. Take care of being under any concern about salvation. There is no need of so much ado about religion and Heaven."

(h) The last mark of the rich man's folly was to say to his deluded soul, "Eat, drink, and be merry"—as if a soul could eat and drink what money can procure or barns contain. No, my brethren, the grace of God and the benefits of Christ's death, which are called His flesh and blood, the bread of life, and the living water, are the only food and drink proper for our souls. And the true mirth and solid joy of a spirit is that to which St. Paul exhorts us: "Rejoice in the Lord, and again I say, rejoice" (Phil. 4:4).

2. The separation between this rich farmer and his all was sudden and unexpected: "This night," said God, "shall thy soul be required of thee." This night; not so much as tomorrow is allowed him to dispose of those goods which were laid up for many years. He must suddenly, immediately part with all.

(a) All his moveable goods—except a winding sheet. (b) All his landed estate—except a grave. (c) All his barns and halls—except a coffin. (d) All his friends and relations, without exception. He must go this dismal journey alone and unattended. (e) All his time, his precious time, which the living kill so many ways, and which the dying and the dead would gladly recover by parting with a world if they had it to part with. (f) His soul, it is to be feared.

Let us here reflect how careful we are to secure our doors lest thieves should break in and take away some of our goods, and yet how careless to provide for death, who carries away all, or rather hurries us away from all at once! What an alarming thought is this for impenitent sinners! May their souls be required this very night? O let them not plot wickedness and contrive vanity against tomorrow.

3. How wonderful is the nature, how inestimable is the value of that soul which was required of this fool, and which shall be required of us! How excellent is that noble, that neglected being, in itself? Spiritual—immortal—endued with the most glorious faculties—made after the very image of God!

How precious is it, as well as how excellent. It is a jewel of inestimable value, and its worth may be estimated (a) From the admirable texture of the body, which is only the casket where that jewel is placed. (b) From the extraordinary pains which the sons of men take to repair and adorn the body, whose value depends only on the jewel it contains. (c) From the testimony of Christ, Who prefers one soul to the whole material creation: "What shall it profit a man if he gain the whole world and lose his own soul?" (Matt. 16:26).

Suffer me then to entreat you, brethren, to bestow pains and care on your souls in some measure proportionable to their worth. At least, be not offended with us ministers for showing some concern for the salvation of your precious, immortal souls.

4. Who shall require his soul? "Thy soul shall be required." The original word means "They shall require." The question then offers itself: Who are they that shall require the unprepared worldling's soul?

I answer: (a) Not Christ as a Savior, for in that capacity He hath nothing to do with dying unbelievers. They would not receive His grace into their hearts, and He will not receive them into His glory (Prov. 1:24). (b) Nor good angels. We read, indeed, that they carried Lazarus to Abraham's bosom (Luke 16:22), but the rich man found his way to the flames without them. (c) Nor departed saints, who neither can nor will meddle with unregenerated souls. For this we may read the conversation between Abraham and the wretch who prayed to him for help (Luke 16). Who then? (a) Some unforeseen accident or distemper. (b) Death, who, as an officer, delivers the wicked into the hands of the tormentors. (c) Evil spirits, the ministers of divine justice, which may be inferred from the strong sense of the powers of darkness which some wicked men have in their last moments. See the case of the memorable Francis Spira.

Believers cheerfully resign their souls into their Savior's hands. Yea, they long to depart and to be with Christ, which is far better. Unbelievers, who have their portion in this world, are loath to leave it; but a peremptory, forcible command shall set aside all their pleas. Their soul shall be required.

5. The last words of the text afford matter for the last head of the discourse. Death comes to require a soul. "Not of me," says, perhaps, the rich farmer, "Not of me, for I have much goods laid up for many years." But God says, "Of thee shall thy soul be required."

What! may not the soul of some poor Lazarus, who pines away in want, sickness, and obscurity, be required first? No, says God, it must be required of thee. May not an old Simeon, who longs to depart in peace, be allowed to die for the rich man? No. His hour is come; of him is his soul required. But perhaps some of the rich man's servants at the feet of his bed may go upon this fatal errand for him? No, says death, he must go himself. Of thee is thy soul required. See all those weeping friends who surround his bed? May not one of them do for death? "No," cries the stern messenger, "my errand is to thee."

Consider the peremptoriness of the inexorable messenger. Gold will not bribe him. Entreaties prevail not. He takes no notice of promises of amendment. Tears melt him not. In spite of physicians and medicine, he does his office, and requires of the worldling his unprepared soul.

The epithet which God fixes on the rich man belongs (a) To all who depend upon many years of life and do not habitually prepare for death. (b) To all, whether rich or poor, who are not rich towards God. (c) Especially to those who, though they have not the conveniences and hardly the necessaries of life, will yet trample on the riches of divine grace and heavenly glory. If the rich worldling was a fool in God's esteem, how doubly foolish are the poor to whom the Gospel is preached in vain?

Ye foolish virgins, ye slumbering souls, awake—arise—trim your lamps! Be wise to salvation. Be as anxious about your eternal as he was for his temporal prosperity. Pull down, not your barns, but your sins. Build not larger houses, but the house that will stand when death beats upon you with all its storms. Never say to your soul, "Soul, take thine ease," until you have an habitation "not made with hands, eternal in the heavens."

Ye who are wise virgins and who are preparing to meet the Bridegroom, apply to your souls, but in a better sense, the words that the rich fool spoke to his soul, "Eat, drink, and be merry." Feed upon the flesh of Christ and drink His blood. That is, believe the Gospel of Jesus; firmly believe that by His cross He redeemed you from sin, death, hell, and the grave. And through faith in Him you will be able to rejoice in the Lord with unspeakable joy and to antedate your Heaven.

I beseech thee, awakened sinner, who tremblest at death and judgment to come, by the prayer of faith, to the Prince of life, that through the value of His death He may take away the sting of death—sin—from thy heart. Steadfastly believe these comfortable words of St. Paul: "He tasted death for every man; that He, through death, might destroy him that had the power of death, that is, the devil; and deliver them who through fear of death were all their lifetime subject to bondage" (Heb. 2:9, 14, 15). If you heartily credit this blessed report, you will find your fears of death changed into longings after it; and with your dying breath you will be able, through mercy, to challenge the king of terrors and to say with the apostle, "O death, where is thy sting? O grave, where is thy victory? Thanks be to God, Who giveth us the victory, through our Lord Jesus Christ."

Index of Correspondents

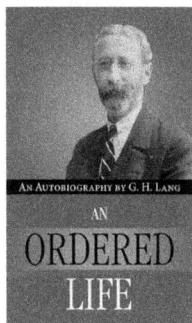

The Revival We Need

by Oswald J. Smith

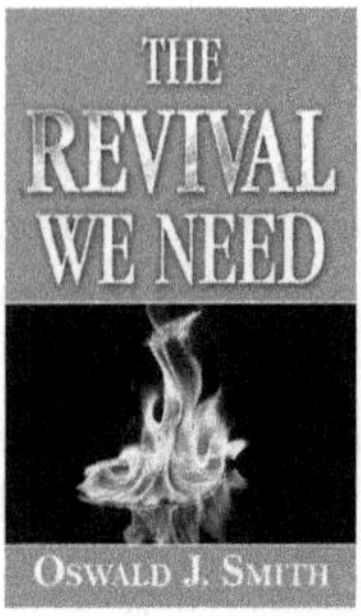

When Oswald J. Smith wrote this book almost a hundred years ago he felt the most pressing need of the worldwide church was true revival—the kind birthed in desperate prayer and accompanied by deep conviction for sin, godly sorrow, and deep repentance, resulting in a living, victorious faith. If he were alive today he would surely conclude that the need has only become more acute with the passing years.

The author relates how there came a time in his own ministry when he became painfully aware that his efforts were not producing spiritual results. His intense study of the New Testament and past revivals only deepened this conviction. The Word of God, which had proved to be a hammer, a fire and a sword in the hands of apostles and revivalists of bygone days, was powerless in his hands. But as he prayed and sought God in dead earnest for the outpouring of the Holy Spirit, things began to change. Souls came under conviction, repented of their sins, and were lastingly changed.

The earlier chapters of the book contain Smith's heart-stirring messages on the need for authentic revival: how to prepare the way for the Spirit's moving, the tell-tale signs that the work is genuine, and the obstacles that can block up the channels of blessing. These chapters are laced with powerful quotations from revivalists and soul-winners of former times, such as David Brainerd, William Bramwell, John Wesley, Charles Finney, Evan Roberts and many others. The latter chapters detail Smith's own quest for the enduement of power, his soul-travail, and the spiritual fruit that followed.

In his foreword to this book, Jonathan Goforth writes, "Mr. Smith's book, *The Revival We Need,* for its size is the most powerful plea for revival I have ever read. He has truly been led by the Spirit of God in preparing it. To his emphasis for the need of a Holy Spirit revival I can give the heartiest amen. What I saw of revival in Korea and in China is in fullest accord with the revival called for in this book."

Buy online at our website: **www.KingsleyPress.com**
Also available as an eBook for Kindle, Nook and iBooks.

Lord, Teach Us to Pray

By Alexander Whyte

Dr. Alexander Whyte (1836-1921) was widely acknowledged to be the greatest Scottish preacher of his day. He was a mighty pulpit orator who thundered against sin, awakening the consciences of his hearers, and then gently leading them to the Savior. He was also a great teacher, who would teach a class of around 500 young men after Sunday night service, instructing them in the way of the Lord more perfectly.

In the later part of Dr. Whyte's ministry, one of his pet topics was prayer. Luke 11:1 was a favorite text and was often used in conjunction with another text as the basis for his sermons on this subject. The sermons printed here represent only a few of the many delivered. But each one is deeply instructive, powerful and convicting.

Nobody else could have preached these sermons; after much reading and re-reading of them that remains the most vivid impression. There can be few more strongly personal documents in the whole literature of the pulpit. . . . When all is said, there is something here that defies analysis—something titanic, something colossal, which makes ordinary preaching seem to lie a long way below such heights as gave the vision in these words, such forces as shaped their appeal. We are driven back on the mystery of a great soul, dealt with in God's secret ways and given more than the ordinary measure of endowment and grace. His hearers have often wondered at his sustained intensity; as Dr. Joseph Parker once wrote of him: "many would have announced the chaining of Satan for a thousand years with less expenditure of vital force" than Dr. Whyte gave to the mere announcing of a hymn. —*From the Preface*

Buy online at our website: **www.KingsleyPress.com**
Also available as an eBook for Kindle, Nook and iBooks.

The Way of the Cross

by J. Gregory Mantle

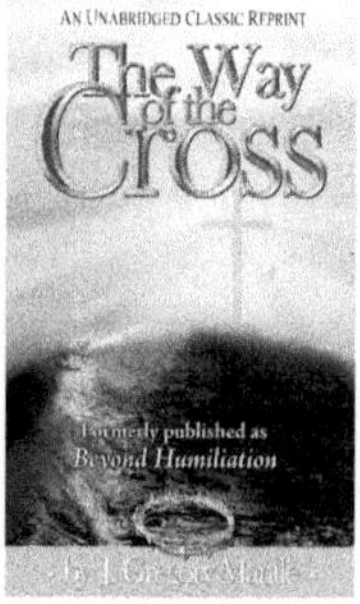

"DYING to self is the *one only way* to life in God," writes Dr. Mantle in this classic work on the cross. "The end of self is the one condition of the promised blessing, and he that is not willing to die to things sinful, *yea, and to things lawful,* if they come between the spirit and God, cannot enter that world of light and joy and peace, provided on this side of heaven's gates, where thoughts and wishes, words and works, delivered from the perverting power of self—revolve round Jesus Christ, as the planets revolve around the central sun. . . .

"It is a law of dynamics that two objects cannot occupy the same space at the same time, and if we are ignorant of the crucifixion of the self-life as an experimental experience, we cannot be filled with the Holy Spirit. 'If thy heart,' says Arndt in his *True Christianity,* 'be full of the world, there will be no room for the Spirit of God to enter; for where the one is the other cannot be.' If, on the contrary, we have endorsed our Saviour's work as the destroyer of the works of the devil, and have claimed to the full the benefits of His death and risen life, what hinders the complete and abiding possession of our being by the Holy Spirit but our unbelief?"

Rev. J. Gregory Mantle (1853 - 1925) *had a wide and varied ministry in Great Britain, America, and around the world. For many years he was the well-loved Superintendent of the flourishing Central Hall in Deptford, England, as well as a popular speaker at Keswick and other large conventions for the deepening of spiritual life. He spent the last twelve years of his life in America, where he was associated with Dr. A. B. Simpson and the Christian and Missionary Alliance. He traveled extensively, holding missions and conventions all over the States. He was an avid supporter of foreign missions throughout his entire career. He also edited a missionary paper, and wrote several books.*

GIPSY SMITH
HIS LIFE AND WORK

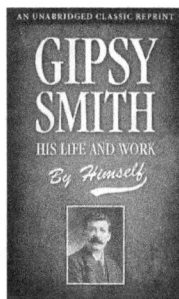

A Present Help

By Marie Monsen

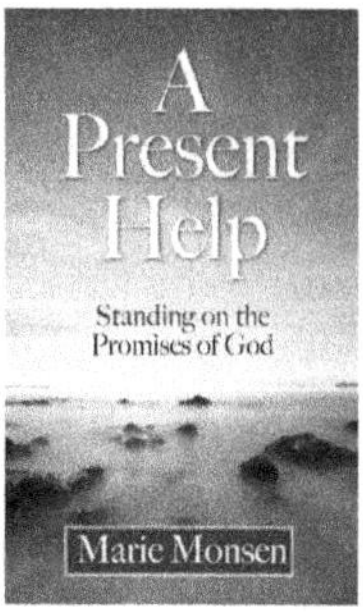

Does your faith in the God of the impossible need reviving? Do you think that stories of walls of fire and hosts of guardian angels protecting God's children are only for Bible times? Then you should read the amazing accounts in this book of how God and His unseen armies protected and guided Marie Monsen, a Norwegian missionary to China, as she traveled through bandit-ridden territory spreading the Gospel of Jesus Christ and standing on the promises of God. You will be amazed as she tells of an invading army of looters who ravaged a whole city, yet were not allowed to come near her mission compound because of angels standing sentry over it. Your heart will thrill as she tells of being held captive on a ship for twenty-three days by pirates whom God did not allow to harm her, but instead were compelled to listen to her message of a loving Savior who died for their sin. As you read the many stories in this small volume your faith will be strengthened by the realization that our God is a living God who can still bring protection and peace in the midst of the storms of distress, confusion and terror—a very present help in trouble.

ANTHONY NORRIS GROVES
SAINT AND PIONEER

by G. H. Lang

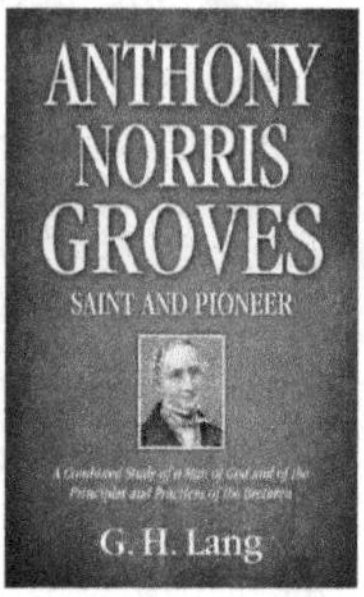

Although his name is little known in Christian cirlces today, Anthony Norris Groves (1795-1853) was, according to the writer of this book, one of the most influential men of the nineteenth century. He was what might be termed a spiritual pioneer, forging a path through unfamiliar territory in order that others might follow. One of those who followed him was George Müller, known to the world as one who in his lifetime cared for over ten thousand orphans without any appeal for human aid, instead trusting God alone to provide for the daily needs of this large enterprise.

In 1825 Groves wrote a booklet called *Christian Devotedness* in which he encouraged fellow believers and especially Christian workers to take literally Jesus' command not to lay up treasures on earth, but rather to give away their savings and possessions toward the spread of the gospel and to embark on a life of faith in God alone for the necessaries of life. Groves himself took this step of faith: he gave away his fortune, left his lucrative dental practice in England, and went to Baghdad to establish the first Protestant mission to Arabic-speaking Muslims. His going was not in connection with any church denomination or missionary society, as he sought to rely on God alone for needed finances. He later went to India also.

His approach to missions was to simplify the task of churches and missions by returning to the methods of Christ and His apostles, and to help indigenous converts form their own churches without dependence on foreign support. His ideas were considered radical at the time but later became widely accepted in evangelical circles.

Groves was a leading figure in the early days of what Robert Govett would later call the mightiest movement of the Spirit of God since Pentecost—a movement that became known simply as the Brethren. In this book G. H. Lang combines a study of the life and influence of Anthony Norris Groves with a survey of the original principles and practices of the Brethren movement.

MEMOIRS OF DAVID STONER

EDITED BY
WILLIAM DAWSON & JOHN HANNAH

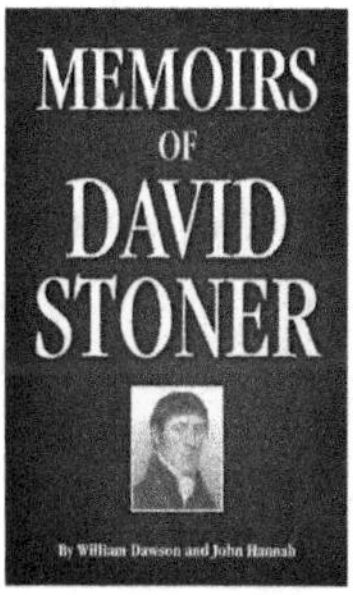

The name of David Stoner (1794-1826) deserves to be ranked alongside those of Robert Murray McCheyne, David Brainerd and Henry Martyn. Like them, he died at a relatively young age; and like them, his life was marked by a profound hunger and thirst for God and intense passion for souls. Stoner was saved at twelve years of age and from that point until his untimely death twenty years later his soul was continually on full stretch for God.

This book tells the story of his short but amazing life: his godly upgringing, his radical conversion, his call to preach, his amazing success as a Wesleyan Methodist preacher, his patience in tribulation and sickness, and his glorious departure to be with Christ forever. Many pages are devoted to extracts from his personal diary which give an amazing glimpse into the heart of one whose desires were all aflame for more of God.

Oswald J. Smith, in his soul-stirring book, *The Revival We Need,* wrote the following: "Have been reading the diary of David Stoner. How I thank God for it! He is another Brainerd. Have been much helped, but how ashamed and humble I feel as I read it! Oh, how he thirsted and searched after God! How he agonized and travailed! And he died at 32."

You, too can be much helped in your spiritual life as you study the life of this youthful saint of a past generation.

"Be instant and constant in prayer. Study, books, eloquence, fine sermons are all nothing without prayer. Prayer brings the Spirit, the life, the power." —*David Stoner*

Buy online at our website: **www.KingsleyPress.com**
Also available as an eBook for Kindle, Nook and iBooks.

The Christian Hero

A Sketch of the Life of Robert Annan

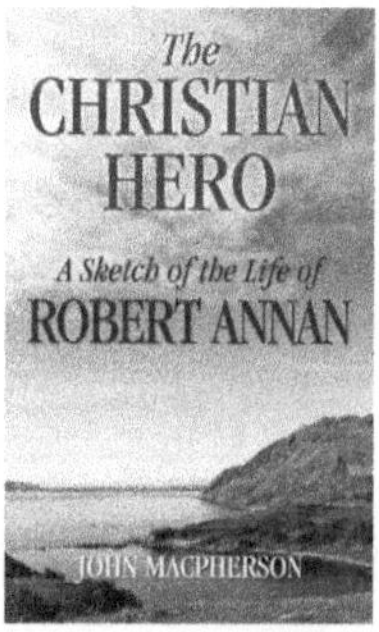

If you've never heard of Robert Annan of Dundee, otherwise known as "the Christian Hero," prepare to be astounded at the amazing grace of God in his life as you turn the pages of this incredible little biography. Its thrilling story will stir you to the depths and almost certainly drive you to your knees with an increased desire to be used for God's glory.

The record of his beginning years reads much like that of John Newton—a life of wandering far from God in the ways of sin and rebellion. At least once he miraculously escaped death through the overruling providence of God. As time passed, he became thoroughly discontented with his sinful life; but he didn't want anything to do with God or Christianity. He thought he could overcome sin and live a morally good life by his own efforts. He soon discovered, however, that he was no match for sin or Satan; and casting himself entirely on God's grace and mercy in Jesus Christ, he was gloriously saved.

From the very first day of his conversion, he became a tireless seeker of lost souls. He worked during the day time as a stone mason, but his evenings and weekends were spent preaching in the streets or in homes. Frequently he would spend whole nights in secret prayer, pleading at the throne of grace for lost sinners. As he went to his employment in the early mornings, he would often write Scripture verses on the pavement for others to read as they passed by on their way to work or school. Thus he was instant in season and out of season, using every opportunity to present to men the claims of Jesus Christ and the reality of heaven, hell, and the judgment that awaits every human soul.

Read his story and be amazed, remembering that what God did for Robert Annan he can and will do for anyone.

Buy online at our website: **www.KingsleyPress.com**
Also available as an eBook for Kindle, Nook and iBooks.

www.ingramcontent.com/pod-product-compliance
Lightning Source LLC
Chambersburg PA
CBHW071957040426
42447CB00009B/1378
* 9 7 8 1 9 3 7 4 2 8 4 7 1 *